PROSECUTED PROSECUTOR

A Memoir & Blueprint for *Prosecutor-led*
Criminal Justice Reform

BIANCA M. **FORDE**

Prosecuted Prosecutor: *A Memoir & Blueprint for* ***Prosecutor-led*** *Criminal Justice Reform*

Copyright © 2020 by Bianca M. Forde

Published By: Forde Ventures, LLC
Website: www.biancaforde.com
Email: info@prosecutedprosecutor.com

Disclaimer: The stories, anecdotes, and case synopses included herein are based on the author's personal encounters and professional experiences. Many names of individuals and parties have been changed to protect privacy and identity. Where dialogue appears, the author has conveyed the essence of the conversations, rather than verbatim accounts.

Cover Design | Caspar Stuart of STU**ART** Design, LLC
Interior Formatting | Molo Global Consulting, LLC

ISBN: 978-1-7357697-0-7 (paperback)
ISBN: 978-1-7357697-1-4 (eBook)
ISBN: 978-1-7357697-2-1 (hardcover)

Library of Congress Control Number: 2020918693

Printed in Washington DC, in the United States of America

For my mother and our good name; for the transformational prosecutor unafraid to disrupt the status quo; for the law enforcement officer ready to confront and acknowledge systemic and implicit bias; and for the voter eager to use the local ballot box to impact change.

For Joseph, my Rehoboth.

CONTENTS

INTRODUCTION

"When I grow up, I want to be a lawyer."

Those were my words at the tender age of six years old. If my maternal grandmother were still here, she would tell you that I was outspoken from the moment I learned to speak. Grandma Lucille, equally astonished and aggravated by my natural tendency to speak my mind or "talk back," as it was described in my Black Caribbean household, would warn me that if I did not mind my tongue as an attorney, I'd be "held in contempt by the magistrate." I suppose she was not too far off.

At age six, I knew nothing about the law, other than what I saw on *Matlock* and *Perry Mason*. As a teenager, I stumbled across a different kind of legal drama inspired by real events, *Law and Order*. It was my introduction to the role of the prosecutor. I was in awe of Jack McCoy's skillful advocacy—the brilliant way that he navigated curveball after legal curveball. I was captivated by his passion for justice, and outrage amidst unjust outcomes. I anticipated his zealous closing arguments, which always seemed to leave the reasonable viewer hard-pressed to find a reason to doubt. My intrigue with trial work and criminal justice would lead me to become a prosecutor one day, but not without detour.

I would spend the early years of my legal career handling

high-stakes commercial disputes and investigations at white-shoe law firms in New York City. My compensation would be high, but my job satisfaction would, at times, be low. I had a gift for advocacy that was being underutilized, when utilized at all. That experience taught me that a life that does not create the space to exercise one's God-given gifts and talents is no life at all. It took me years to muster the courage to leave my big-law career and all of its perks behind; but in 2015, I did just that. In September of that year, I was inducted into the prestigious ranks of federal prosecution. I'd been told that it would be the best job in the world, and in many ways, it has been.

After three weeks of basic training, I was assigned to the Misdemeanor Domestic Violence ("MDV") Trial Section. There, I met young men and women—mostly young Black women—who had been abused, mistreated, disrespected and violated in ways that troubled my soul. I felt an instant connection to many of them, and began to realize how important it was for my relationship with these women to be more than that of prosecutor and victim. For many of them, I was the first self-sufficient, educated Black woman they had ever met. I would be the first person to ever speak up for them, without requesting anything in return. I would be their voice. Because of my time in MDV, there will always be a special place in my heart for victims of domestic violence crimes. I believe there are few greater betrayals than being intentionally harmed by the ones we love; as such, there are few callings more noble than seeking justice on behalf of those so harmed.

My experience has also taught me that the term "victim" is by no means static. As a rookie prosecutor, I considered my victims to be blameless. "*My victim*"—a phrase that prosecutors often use, but ought not to—was the person deserving of justice. *My victim* was the one hurt, bloodied and bruised, the one who had been betrayed. As a result of this mindset, in mere months, I became frustrated by the frequency with which judges in MDV cases imposed "suspended sentences." Suspended sentences, or the "Execution of Sentence Suspended", colloquially referred to as *ESS-all*, typically involve an exchange between the judge and the defendant, similar to the fictive depiction below:

Judge: Mr. Smith, I've just found you guilty of the crime of simple assault. The statute provides for a maximum penalty of 180 days. The government has asked for 100 days of incarceration, and your attorney has asked for 10 days. As this is your first contact with the criminal justice system, I will impose a sentence of 60 days; but I will suspend all of that time, and place you on probation for one year. That means the 60-day period of incarceration that I have imposed will hang over your head, so to speak.

If you stay out of trouble for the length of your probationary period, you will be free and clear. If you are rearrested, or convicted of any other offense, I will impose all of that time and you will spend 60 days in jail. Do you understand?

Mr. Smith: Yes, Your Honor.

In my early days as a prosecutor, I loathed *ESS-all*, especially when imposed by judges in cases involving repeat domestic violence offenders. I hated *ESS-all* because it seemed insufficient, both as a deterrent, and as punishment, for repeat offenders. I would often rant to my sister, Allana, "How can this be justice? Probation is not going to stop Mr. Smith from putting his hands on *my victim*." Allana, who had spent years as a public defender, and was much wiser and more experienced on the matter than I, was the first to explain what my experience would ultimately teach me. The terms *victim*, *witness,* and *defendant* are fluid. Today's *defendant* is tomorrow's *victim*. "It's not as black and white as you think," she cautioned me; she was absolutely right.

Since then, I have had the privilege of prosecuting a wide variety of criminal cases at the local and federal levels. I have investigated and tried cases involving arson, corruption & bribery, financial fraud, sexual assault, shootings, violent assaults, robbery, burglary, homicide, and possessory gun and drug offenses. Through such cases, I have seen firsthand what Allana had expressed years before—there is simply nothing black and white about the complex variety of factors that put a person on a path into the criminal justice system. Quite the contrary, all roads connected to the justice system in America are paved in gray. The ability to recognize and interpret the *gray* is essential to the role of the prosecutor, and directly impacts how prosecutorial discretion is exercised. However, *gray* is a concept that is exceedingly difficult to teach. Little did I know, that once again, experience would be my most profound and effective teacher.

I was privy to the *gray* long before my arrest; however, the juxtaposition of being both prosecutor and prosecuted, underscored the myriad of ways in which the U.S. criminal justice system dehumanizes and mishandles those entangled in it. I have come to realize that—if we are not careful—prosecutors can become a conduit for such mistreatment, especially early on in our careers; and bad habits, once learned, are hard to break. I have learned that the hand of justice swings most heavily when young, inexperienced prosecutors are at the table. In a provocative piece titled, *The Cure for Young Prosecutors' Syndrome*, Professors Ronald Wright and Kay L. Levin posit that:

> Promoting balance for young prosecutors could be the most important single step our criminal justice system can

take to improve its health and sustainability. Because of the absence of functional checks and balances in criminal charging and sentencing, prosecutor decisions are central to any effort to restore balance to a bloated and expensive prison system that is far out of proportion to historic and international comparison points.[i]

In other words, if you have never prosecuted the homicide of a known murderer, gained the trust of a crack addict to make a case, or sought dismissal of a proceeding for reasons unrelated to whether a crime occurred, you may be prone to view *victims*, *defendants* and *witnesses* in static and over simplified terms. You may consciously or unconsciously assign values such as "good" and "bad" to the terms *victim* and *defendant*, respectively. You may even view the accused as no different from the conduct alleged against them, and therefore deserving of whatever consequences come their way; but with experience comes insight. With exposure, you learn that no person should be reduced to "the worst thing they have ever done."[ii] This insight fundamentally alters one's perspective of, and thus behavior toward, the person on the other side of the "v."

The experienced prosecutor understands that, sometimes, a scorned ex fabricates allegations for revenge. The street-savvy prosecutor knows when there is more to a story than what a victim or witness is choosing to reveal. The mature prosecutor understands that police officers don't always tell the truth. Understanding what to do in these situations requires a level of discernment that the inexperienced prosecutor lacks. So imagine my disappointment when I learned that the prosecutor assigned to my case was just three months out of law school. Imagine my fear that she had not yet learned the *gray*. Imagine my concern, that to her, I would simply be the person on the other side of the "v."

It is generally accepted that prosecutors are the most powerful actors in the criminal justice system. In one of our generation's most brilliant expositions on race and justice, Michelle Alexander declares that it is the American prosecutor who "holds the keys to the jail-house door."[iii] Unfortunately, many prosecutors are assigned their first case without understanding the power that they wield, or the tangible way in which even the most routine act of prosecutorial discretion directly impacts life, liberty and justice. In this book, I aim to bridge this knowledge gap and fast-forward the learning curve of the rookie prosecutor. I invite discourse on the too-taboo-to-touch topics that have undermined the American justice system for far too long. I identify my early mistakes as well as my evolution; I do all of this in an attempt to teach the *gray*.

Part One describes my personal encounter with the criminal justice system, and illustrates the countless ways in which the U.S. criminal justice system is uniquely designed to strip away the humanity of all who come in contact with it. Part Two examines the complexity of simultaneously being both prosecuted and prosecutor, and explains how my arrest, and its aftermath, positioned me to recognize that the justice I sought to uphold as a prosecutor, was being constantly undermined by policies and practices implemented by powerful decision-makers who had never learned the *gray*. Part Three educates and empowers prosecutors to use their vast power to inspire meaningful, lasting change, while edifying civic-minded community members on how to identify and elect prosecutors capable of real transformation.

The framework provided in this book is meant to disrupt the status quo. It sets forth practical lessons that can be implemented right away by both new and veteran prosecutors. It imparts perspectives that some prosecutors only develop after years on the job, and sadly, others never develop at all. Meanwhile, millions of charged individuals unwittingly pay the price of becoming the involuntary guinea pigs of the prosecutor's professional development journey.

This book is my gift to a system that has both trained me and betrayed me; it is a critique of the job I once blindly loved, but can no longer be satisfied with, if the system remains in its present state. This book is a blueprint for achieving a fair, balanced, and compassionate justice system through justice-minded prosecution. It is a call to action. If mass incarceration is in fact the new civil rights movement,[iv] then prosecutors must lead the next wave of criminal justice reform. While some are of the mindset that good people should not be prosecutors and, instead, choose to advance the harmful narrative that it is impossible to transform the system from within, I dare you to imagine a system where the good and justice-minded are excluded from the ranks of prosecution.

This book is for those courageous enough to confront our own biases; those open-minded enough to consider the possibility that justice, as we know it, is not always just. This book is for all of us who grew up to become the advocates we always wanted to be, impassioned and unafraid to "talk back" when the stakes are too high to mind our tongues.

PART ONE: THE DIVINE DISRUPTION

"God will allow your entire life to be disrupted to push purpose out of you."

—DIETTA RODDIE

CHAPTER 1: EIGHTEEN HOURS

"Burn it down."

Those words were carved into the locked iron door of my 5-by-5-foot cell, equipped with nothing but a hard wooden bench. As I sat there for hours—waiting—those words stared back at me. *Burn it down.* If I didn't know what they meant when I walked into the Seventh Police Precinct around midnight on November 29, 2019, I would most certainly learn.

In a locked jail cell, minutes can feel like hours; hours can feel like days. I spent eighteen hours in the Department of Corrections ("DOC") custody during Thanksgiving weekend of 2019. Eighteen hours of waiting; eighteen hours of asking questions that were ignored; eighteen hours of being told to speak to my "arresting officer", whose name was not readily given to me; eighteen hours of being treated as subhuman; eighteen hours on benches unsuitable for sitting, much less sleeping; eighteen hours of trying to avoid human feces spread all over the walls; eighteen hours where my only amenities were a traffic mirror that allowed me to observe the comings and goings around the cellblock, and a locked computer screen that displayed the time; eighteen hours in a holding cell—when the officer that arrested me could have, instead, given me a ticket with a court date, sort of like the one given to "Central Park Karen"; eighteen hours of waiting to be "processed."

To be "processed" means to be handled. That is what those involved in the process do. They handle you; they handle you by ignoring you; they handle you by giving you false, or incomplete information—for example, claiming that you have been charged with a felony, when you have actually been charged with a misdemeanor; they handle you by using every possible opportunity to flex their power; they handle you by treating you as though you do not matter; your questions do not matter; your basic need to know what is happening does not matter. As human beings, we are built to want information, to seek clarity, to have an understanding of what will happen next. It is not until those basic needs are unmet, that we realize how essential they are to our sanity, and to our peace of mind.

As I sat there in that locked jail cell, powerless, knowing my needs were irrelevant to all in proximity, and with the authority to meet them, I thought about my future or what was left of it. I clung to my amenities, the clock and traffic mirror, the latter offering an occasional distraction from my personal plight—starting with Isis.

I can still remember seeing Isis for the first time. I heard her long before I saw her. She was sobbing uncontrollably. I couldn't help but wonder what unfortunate stream of events landed her in this N.Y.C. precinct. Speculating about her troubles momentarily took my mind off of my own. Amidst her sobs, I heard the clanking of metal, the sound of keys entering the iron cellblock keyhole. My eyes locked in on the traffic mirror. The door slid open, and there she was.

She was as young as her tears and weeping suggested she might be, definitely in her early twenties or so. She looked to be ethnic; not Latina, but perhaps something exotic. Growing up in Long Island, you were either Black, White, or "Spanish." Spanish was the term used to describe anyone Spanish-speaking, regardless of nationality. Through life and exposure, I would learn that the term "Spanish" should be reserved for those actually born in Spain. In any event, I could tell Isis was not Black, White, or Spanish-speaking. I'd later learn that she was of Egyptian descent.

Isis was wearing black, ripped denim jeans, a matching denim jacket and a body suit, with a full face of runny make-up. *"She must have been out and about when she was arrested,"* I thought. From the intensity of her crying, it was clear that jail was no more her norm than it was mine—which was a good thing, considering we'd likely be sharing a cell for quite some time. If I'd learned anything from *Orange is the New Black*, and the scores of other televised dramas about life behind bars, I had learned not to show weakness. Isis had apparently missed those broadcasts.

The cellblock had two large holding cells—one for men and one for women. When I arrived, there was one man in the male holding cell. By the time I left, there were several. Luckily, I would have the women's holding cell all to myself, that is, until Isis finally joined me. I continued to wonder why Isis was even there. Maybe she was holding drugs or a gun for some guy she fancied; maybe she'd gotten into a fight and was there on an assault charge; or maybe she had the gall to question two fragile-ego officers, who thought it fit to flex their muscle and manhood by placing her in cuffs. *Oh, no wait, that was me!*

I watched intently as a female officer escorted Isis, still sobbing hysterically, to the cellblock toilet. There was only one toilet for the men and women to share. It appeared to not have been cleaned in days, possibly longer. Soon thereafter, Isis and the officer began to walk toward the women's holding cell. I felt a wave of relief, believing I would soon have some company; someone to talk to, someone who was in a position to acknowledge my humanity, unlike those beyond the bars. Raised by a single-mother, and as my mother's only child, this sudden, all-encompassing need for company was new and unfamiliar to me. Yet, I welcomed the thought of having a cellmate—a non-threatening one of course, and Isis fit the bill.

This wave of relief, however, was short-lived. Just as the female officer began to unlock the women's holding cell door, a male voice echoed through the cellblock, "Take her to the room!" "Already?" the female officer responded, quizzically. "Yes," the male voice confirmed. Immediately, the female officer turned Isis around, directed her toward the cellblock door, and—in a matter of seconds—the two were gone. I was alone again. Except for the rapidly growing number of male arrestees in the adjacent holding cell, I was left to quietly, and restlessly, wonder about Isis and this mysterious room.

Where was this room? What was in this room, and why did Isis get to go there? More importantly—why did she get to go there so quickly? Clearly, I had been sitting here alone for at least an hour, but I hadn't been taken to "the room." Would I be taken to "the room" at some point? And, if so, when? What happens in "the room?" Are there lawyers in "the room?" Are arrestees interviewed in "the room?" The questions in my head were relentless, but they were all I had as I sat and waited to be handled, watching the minutes slowly advance on the locked computer screen in front of me, listening for any indication of what was going on beyond the locked iron door, and beyond the traffic mirror's view.

Finally, there was some activity. Keys jingling near the door and Isis sobbing more intensely than before. "*What on earth could have happened in that room?*" I thought. The cellblock door opened and a male officer now escorted Isis back towards the women's holding cell, but first, another trip to the toilet. Isis continued to weep, but now she was dry heaving and vomiting. I wondered what brought on this vomiting. *Was it alcohol-induced, or something else? Lord, please don't leave me in here with a crack head!* Suddenly, the thought of having a cellmate was less comforting than before. After a few minutes of expelling fluids and feelings, Isis turned the faucet on. I locked in on the traffic mirror, and watched her walk reticently toward the cell we were destined to share. I would soon know exactly what kind of vomiting this had been.

We were all given the option to either take off our shoes, or remove our shoelaces, before entering the cell — a safety measure designed to ensure that no one hung themselves while on the DOC's watch. Isis opted to take her shoes off. I couldn't understand why. She must not have noticed the sheer nastiness of this place. I, on the other hand, did notice, and there was no way my shoes were coming off. God knows there was no reason to assume that the person who spread shit on the walls took caution to avoid the floor.

Now wearing only multi-colored, ankle socks, Isis turned toward the cell and peeked inside. She looked at me and instantly started to wail. I was not offended; I knew exactly what she was thinking because I had been thinking the exact same thing—*God, please don't let this chick be crazy.* I decided to offer her a little comfort, "I promise you, I'm not scary, hon." Her escort, who would eventually become *our* escort—I'll call him the "Transport Officer"—seconded my assurances to Isis. In the end, the Transport Officer would stand out as one of the kinder policemen that I encountered during my eighteen hours in custody that weekend, although the bar was low. The Transport Officer then unlocked the cell door, allowing Isis to enter.

Isis stepped in slowly. Her face was now a canvas of mixed colors, the remnants of her black mascara being most prominent. Before he could close and lock the door, I asked the Transport

Officer to allow me to use the toilet. As I approached the stall, I could smell Isis's vomit before I even walked inside. It was overpowering, but what was I going to do? Hold it?

Before heading back to the holding cell, I grabbed some extra tissues for Isis, who was still inconsolable. As I handed them to her, we made eye contact and she let out another loud sob. However, this one was different. It was as if in that moment, she knew that I wasn't crazy, dangerous or scary. I was just another young woman who neither expected, nor deserved, to spend the Friday after Thanksgiving, or any night for that matter, in a jail cell.

With that realization, it did not take long for Isis to open up to me. Once she started talking, I felt as though she would never stop. Isis had been arrested for reckless driving. She explained that she was with a girlfriend when the police stopped her. For hours, she complained that her girlfriend had simply abandoned her after the arrest. We later learned that the friend had spent the entire night in the precinct waiting for Isis's release. Isis explained that she was going through a break-up, and attributed her emotional state to her romantic troubles as opposed to her legal ones. She even quenched my curiosity about the mysterious room. The room was designed for sobriety tests. Isis's sobriety test was inconclusive in the field, so the officers were trying their hand again.

Isis also had a lot of questions. To the extent that I could answer them, I did. It made her wonder how I knew so much and why I was so calm. She assumed I'd been arrested before and had become familiar, maybe even comfortable, with the process. What she did not know, and what I was not inclined to share, was that the true source of my knowledge was several years of experience as a federal prosecutor.

After some time had passed, Isis invited me to lay my head on her shoulder. I hesitated. She was still a stranger, and, in any event, I wondered, *"were we past the vomiting?"* Eventually, I stopped fighting the fatigue. She laid her head on my shoulder, and I laid my head on hers. She was, after all, the safest and most sanitary pillow available to me. We talked until she fell asleep. I desperately wanted to do the same, but I could not shut my mind off. I resigned myself to lying awake on that hard, wooden bench, trying desperately not to touch the feces-covered walls.

CHAPTER 2: UNRULY BLACK WOMAN

Around 3:00 a.m. or so, another officer entered the cellblock, I'll call him the "Processing Officer." He was tall, African-American, and in his mid-forties. It was not the first time I'd seen this officer. He was in the precinct lobby when I first arrived. He was having an angry exchange with a citizen who appeared to have returned to the precinct, post release, to retrieve his personal property. I do not know what prompted the angry exchange, but the two yelled back and forth as I stood there in tears watching the Arresting Officer— the most aggressive of them all—unconstitutionally search and inventory my things. Someone definitely needed to train this squad of officers on the concept of de-escalation.

By the time the Processing Officer entered the cellblock, Isis was sound asleep. I, on the other hand, was hopelessly awake with my thoughts. I thought about my mother, a single parent, to whom I owed it all. What would her reaction be to my arrest? She had literally sacrificed everything to make sure that I could benefit from every educational opportunity available to me. Up until this point, I had made her so proud. Whatever little she had, she invested in me. All of her delayed dreams had been implicitly deferred to me. Yet, there I was, in the last place she would ever expect for me to be—a jail cell.

I thought about statistics, in particular about Black women being the fastest growing members of the jail and prison population. A recent study concluded that one in eighteen Black women would find themselves detained during their lifetime.[i] Another illustrated that Black women are arrested roughly three times more than White women during police-initiated stops.[ii] I'd made it thirty-five years without being a "statistic," yet there I was; I had nineteen years of schooling, yet there I was; I was a lawyer and a federal prosecutor, yet there I was; I was not *just* a federal prosecutor—I was one who worked earnestly and tirelessly to uphold and protect the integrity of the system; yet, there I was.

Several months before my arrest, I was elected to serve as Eastern Regional Director of the National Black Prosecutors Association (NBPA). NBPA was founded in Chicago in 1983 to focus on the hiring, retention, and advancement of Black prosecutors. The birth of the organization symbolized a lack of diversity in a space that so directly impacts life and liberty, in particular, the life and liberty of those who identify as Black in America. Indeed, as recently as 2014, 95% of elected prosecutors were White.[iii] NBPA had become virtually invisible in the Washington, D.C. Metro Area, the "DMV," which was shocking given the number of Black prosecutors in the region. I was passionate about reviving NBPA in the DMV. I was even more passionate about changing the pervasive negative narrative regarding prosecution by attracting justice-minded lawyers and students into the fold, and reminding current prosecutors of their power, and their responsibility to use that power for good. Yet here I was, one of eighteen, treated and handled as though I was public enemy number one—simply because I chose to use my voice.

I've learned that people tend to treat others how they see them. That weekend, the officers I encountered saw me through the lens that has been used to frame Black women for centuries. I was not assertive; I was aggressive. I was not intelligent; I was emasculating. I was not feminine; I was a threat. In *The Violent State: Black Women's Invisible Struggle Against Police Violence*, Michelle S. Jacobs asks rhetorically, whether it is possible that increased violence and hostility toward Black women can be attributed to an officer's perceived threat to his masculinity when face-to-face with Black women.[iv] "Of Course," she explains:

> [I]t is possible to envision a scenario where Black women would indeed create a threat to a police officer's masculinity. One of the popular stereotypes about Black women that is repeated in media, in advertising, and in development of both social welfare policy as well as criminal justice policy, is the version of the overbearing, demeaning Black woman, who emasculates men. When police officers see Black women who may not verbally submit readily to them, it could present a masculinity threat to them, thus triggering excessive use of force against the women.[v]

After reading Jacobs's work, my November 2019 encounter with N.Y.P.D. made more sense. From the outset, I knew that my partner and I had been profiled; and I was confident that, had I been an outspoken White woman, I would not have seen the inside of a jail cell that night. However, Jacobs helped me to understand and articulate *why* the officers were so quick to place me in cuffs. From their perspective, who was I to question their authority, their legitimacy, and their exercise of discretion? This unruly Black woman deserved to pay; and so I did.

During those eighteen hours, I saw my entire future flash before my eyes countless times. I saw my dreams for myself, and my mother's dreams for me, flushed down the cellblock's vomit-filled toilet. While Isis lay on my shoulder, peacefully asleep—an obvious escape from reality—anger kept my synapses sharp. And dear God was I angry. I was angry at how I had been treated, disrespected, and handled; but I was also afraid. I was afraid that those with the power to decide what would happen next in my career would not understand how a traffic stop ended with my arrest.

I would spend the ride from Hell's Kitchen to the Seventh Precinct contemplating how I would inform my superiors about my predicament, naively believing that they would learn about the ordeal directly from me. Little did I know that there was such a shortage of newsworthy material that evening that my little arrest would become national news. I had no idea that, by the time of my release, my face—and a sensationalized version of the incident—would be blasted across multiple media outlets under click-bait headlines. I was mortified when I learned over a prison pay phone that the New York Post had published a story about my arrest and, moreover, had already called my office for comment.

If the headlines weren't bad enough, some of the comments were worse. It was clear that many who commented had resorted to "twitter fingers" without reading the articles' text. However, there were comments of support as well. People close to me began sending the positive ones as a source of encouragement. I was moved when Soledad O'Brien tweeted about my story. I was overcome with emotion when the Lawyers' Committee for Civil Rights did the same, tweeting that "she knew her rights and was arrested for it." It was nice to know that there were people who saw the encounter for what it was.

Still, it saddened me to become national news due to an arrest, and to be portrayed as angry, defiant, and unruly.[vi] It was clear that life would never be the same.

CHAPTER 3: A TIME FOR ANSWERS

The Bible says, "to everything, there is a season . . . a time to keep silence and a time to speak."[i] After hours of silently processing, the time had come to speak. I had questions and I needed answers, beginning with *what was I charged with and when would I see a judge?*

I had never practiced criminal law in New York, so there was a lot that I did not know with respect to process. Still, there are many aspects of criminal law that are presumed standard throughout the United States—certain rights granted by the Constitution, made applicable to the states through the Fourteenth Amendment. One such right is the right to be presented to (e.g., have your case reviewed by) a judge following an arrest. I knew that I was entitled to see a judge within forty-eight hours, even though there was absolutely no reason why it should take that long. In D.C., we strive for twenty-four hours absent special circumstances. I hoped New York would be the same, but I did not know for sure.

I waited patiently for another officer to re-enter the cellblock, so that I could gain some clarity on my situation. The Processing Officer returned within the hour and my barrage of questions began. "Excuse me, officer," I said, "what time does arraignment court start?" He explained that the judge usually takes the bench around 7:30 a.m., or 8:00 a.m., but usually does not start calling cases until closer to 9:00 a.m., or so. "*Not bad*," I thought.

Arraignments in D.C. Superior Court, the venue for local prosecutions, begin in Courtroom C-10 at 1:00 p.m., and continue until every person arrested during the prior 24-hour period, generally speaking, is seen by the judge. For AUSAs (Assistant U.S. Attorneys) in the U.S. Attorney's Office for the District of Columbia ("USAO-DC"), C-10 was arguably one of the least desirable assignments within our local prosecuting division. In most jurisdictions, an elected local District Attorney or State's Attorney handles local matters. In the District of Columbia, the U.S. Attorney—appointed by the president—is responsible for local and federal adult prosecutions, with certain limited exceptions. The ability to handle local and federal cases within one prosecuting office made the U.S. Attorney's Office for the District of Columbia extremely unique.

I figured, since New York's arraignment court began so much earlier than arraignments in D.C., I might have the good fortune of being released by lunch. I continued to probe the Processing Officer. "So, what time do we head to the courthouse?" I asked. "Soon," he replied, the quintessential non-answer. He was handling me again. Surely, this was not his first day on the job. There must have been a window within which transport to the courthouse regularly began. Further, it was New York City. One would imagine that measures would be taken to initiate and/ or complete transport prior to rush hour traffic. However, this officer was not inclined to offer clarity. My need to know would not be met by the Processing Officer at any point during that encounter. That would have been too kind.

At some point, I would learn more about how N.Y.C. arraignment court was structured. Court began around 9:00 a.m., as the Processing Officer indicated. There was a lunch break from 1:00 p.m. to 2:00 p.m., which was immediately followed by an afternoon session. The afternoon session would end at 5:00 p.m., which was when night court began. Night court would then break from 9:00 p.m. to 10:00 p.m., and then continue without interruption until 1:00 am. I tried not to consider the possibility that I could be legally held for that long, but policing my thoughts was proving to be rather difficult.

Having no clear answer on when we would leave the Seventh Precinct, I had no choice but to wait. As painful as it was, I kept watching the clock. I would turn my head away and try to get lost in my thoughts, only to look back and realize that mere minutes had passed. It was borderline unbearable. *How could I make the time go faster? What could I think about? What thoughts could I get lost in? Could I fall asleep? How amazing would it be to close my eyes and wake up to the sound of the cell door opening?* I wanted to fall asleep almost as much as I wanted to be released.

The officers claimed that I had been intoxicated. Intoxicated people pass out in jail cells. Those angry at how their rights have been trampled upon stay awake, fuming. I wanted it all to be a dream, but it most certainly was not. I never fell asleep that night. I did not have the pleasure of forgetting where I was, not for one moment. But a male arrestee, we'll call him Samuel Johnson, offered a welcome distraction.

CHAPTER 4: UNCONSTITUTIONAL SHENANIGANS

You can learn a great deal about another person through the walls of an adjacent jail cell. Samuel Johnson had been the subject of a traffic stop. He'd been pulled over with the mother of his child, who was in the passenger seat of the vehicle. If his cellblock behavior was any indication, Johnson was likely anything but cooperative on scene. He was angry and, the more I involuntarily listened to him, the more I understood why.

The officers that arrested Johnson had taken possession of all of his personal property, even his car. From Johnson's perspective, they could have released his belongings to his child's mother. After all, she was not arrested. There was no reason for the officers to take possession of his car, his cash, or any of his belongings. Yet, this was a common police tactic—a pretext for uncovering evidence of a crime, even in the absence of facts or reasonable suspicion that any crime had occurred. And, while I was not in a position to express my frustration with this practice as vehemently as Johnson could, I certainly understood his position.

Like Johnson, I too, was arrested in the presence of my partner. I was charged with obstructing governmental administration "OGA" for allegedly interfering with the officers' ability to administer a Breathalyzer test. I was also charged with resisting arrest. Neither of these charges, nor any other fact, gave the officers reason to suspect that I was armed, or in possession of any contraband; yet the Arresting Officer, entered our car anyway. He removed my purse—which was not on my person at the time of my arrest, anyway; he rummaged through my purse and all of its contents, anyway. And he did all of this under the pretense that my purse had been in my "grabbable reach" at the time of my arrest. However, as explained below, his definition of "grabbable reach" is completely inconsistent with the legal meaning of the phrase.

The Supreme Court has confirmed two justifications for searching a vehicle without a warrant during a traffic stop.[i] The first is when officers reasonably believe the car contains evidence relevant to the crime of arrest.[ii] For example, imagine that during a traffic stop, an officer observes a small glass vial with liquid and tobacco leaves—a common indicator of possession or usage of liquid Phencyclidine (PCP). In that case, a judge would likely conclude that probable cause existed to search all passenger compartments of the vehicle that could contain PCP. That includes the trunk, glove compartment, center console, carrying cases of any size, etc.

The second instance in which officers may search a vehicle without a warrant, incident to an occupant's arrest, occurs when the arrestee is "unsecured and within reaching distance" (e.g., grabbable reach) of the interior compartments of the car.[iii] The theory is that for their own protection, the officers may search areas within the car that may contain weapons; e.g. - knives, guns, etc. In sum, routine traffic stops do not give officers carte blanche to search a car absent reason to suspect contraband, or justifiable fear for officer safety.[iv] In addition, the Supreme Court has expressly condemned searches of vehicle compartments when it is "improbable" that an arrestee could gain access to

[the] vehicle, [because, for example] he has been handcuffed and secured in the backseat of a patrol car."[v]

So, if the nature of my arrest did not give the officers a legal basis to believe that our car contained contraband, and if I was already handcuffed and secured in the backseat of the transport vehicle when the search occurred, what legal basis did the Arresting Officer have to enter our car, take custody of—and later search—my belongings? How could it be that after being detained, handcuffed, and placed in a squad car with the door closed and locked, I could look up and see my purse sitting on the hood of the N.Y.P.D. transport vehicle? It felt like a good time to speak, so I asked:

"Why did you take my bag?" The squad car door was closed, the window barely open, and the only person interested in anything I had to say was Joseph, my partner.

"*Babe*! Ask them why they have my bag! My bag was not on me!" An officer approached the squad car and I redirected my attention toward him. "Why did y'all take my bag?" I was livid. It was like something out of a movie. Surely, this was not happening. Certainly, these idiots had not entered our car and removed my bag without consent and without a warrant. The rookie officer replied, "Because it was in your grabbable area." *Bullshit!*

When Joseph asked the same question, he was told the bag was my "personal property and had to go with [me]." The term "personal property" in everyday parlance generally refers to anything a person owns. However, in the context of an arrest, the term "personal property" is far more limited and refers only to those things that are physically on the body or person of the arrestee; e.g. in her hands or pockets, at the time of arrest. Certainly, my purse, which never left the passenger floorboard of the car, was not on my person at the time of my arrest.

So, right now you should be wondering why these officers would take my purse. They took my purse for the same reason they took Johnson's car. They took my purse so that they could conduct what is called an "inventory search." Such a search allows an officer to examine and record all of an arrestee's property. The Arresting Officer took my purse, despite having no legal or constitutional basis to do so, and used terms like "grabbable reach" and "personal property" to justify the intrusion, so that he could engage in a fishing expedition designed to spy incriminating evidence that bears no relevance to the alleged basis for the arrest.

That night, when the Arresting Officer made the decision to unconstitutionally enter our car, take possession of my purse, and search it without a warrant in flagrant abuse of his power, he did this because he hoped he would find contraband on me. In the absence of contraband, he or his comrades chose to release my arrest to the press. The Arresting Officer then used my Department of Justice identification to complete his paperwork and, in documents submitted to the court, he lied. He claimed that I had verbally identified myself as a "U.S. Attorney" — a false allegation that I would find more troubling than the criminal charges against me. It was an allegation that could destroy my credibility and reputation, an allegation that would require conversations with Department of Justice (DOJ) officials, who would then be charged with assessing my fitness to be an AUSA. It was an allegation belied by body-worn camera evidence relevant to my case; but one that the Manhattan DA's office allowed to remain in the public record, nonetheless.

I say all of that to say; I understood Johnson's frustration. He was not legally trained, but he knew protocol, and he had every right to be upset. If N.Y.P.D. impounded his car, they could and most certainly would, conduct an inventory search. Why give the car to the girlfriend if the officers had a *hunch* that the car might contain drugs? Why release Johnson's cash to the passenger, if it could later be used as evidence of intent to distribute those same drugs? The inventory search is one of the many ways that the police have been able to work around, rather than abide by, the Constitution.

Unfortunately, while Johnson's anger was entirely justified, his manner of expression was unhelpful. He yelled, hollered, banged on the iron bars, and refused to submit to any routine processing requirements. I'd seen this kind of behavior before—usually in C-10 or some other court proceeding where the behavior was merely disruptive, frustrating, and an impediment to the next part of my day. Observing and relating to it from an adjacent jail cell afforded greater opportunities for empathy.

CHAPTER 5: MY CELLBLOCK PRAYER

Hours had now passed since the Processing Officer told me that we would be heading to see a judge "soon." It was 6:00 a.m., and it appeared that the next phase of processing was about to begin. We had to be fingerprinted and photographed before heading to the courthouse. I knew that my prints were already in the system. I had submitted to an extensive background check before becoming a prosecutor. But this was no SF-86 form.

One of the male arrestees was first to be processed. Not Johnson, who was still refusing to cooperate; another guy who appeared to be coming down from a high or waking up from a very good nap. He had not been allowed to wear a belt in the cell, so his pants were dangerously close to permitting indecent exposure. Unfortunately, the space where processing took place was directly in my line of sight. I would be happy when this young man returned to his cell, where his private parts would be out of my view.

I was next. As the Processing Officer lifted and pressed my fingers and palms against the device that would record my prints, I knew nothing about this was a dream. I now had an arrest record. I would soon have a mug shot. I hoped I wouldn't look like some hardened criminal. *"Oh God, please don't let my mug shot be Googleable,"* I thought. Next, the Processing Officer would direct me toward a wall where I'd stand to have my photo taken. I already knew where to stand; this wasn't rocket science after all. As he manipulated the camera, he instructed me not to show teeth—a pointless admonition. What in the world was there to smile about? I took the opportunity to get clarity on the charges filed against me. The Processing Officer advised that I'd been charged with "felony OGA," as there is no misdemeanor equivalent. I felt my heart sink. *"Why would I be charged with a felony?"* I inquired. The Processing Officer did not respond.

I was not familiar with New York's bail laws, but I knew they were more conservative than the laws in D.C. I also knew that there was a greater chance that I would be held if charged with a felony. I might even be asked to post bail. New York City was notorious for housing thousands of pretrial detainees merely due to an inability to post bail. While in private practice, I represented a pro bono client and Rikers inmate in a civil rights case against the N.Y.C. Department of Corrections. That young man had been detained pretrial for years. So, I knew enough to be afraid of being charged with a felony in New York. I knew that a felony charge meant my release would be less imminent.

The District of Columbia is different. D.C. is perhaps one of the most liberal jurisdictions in terms of bail reform. For several decades, the law in D.C. has maintained that no person be detained simply by virtue of an inability to post bail. Arrestees in D.C. are detained pretrial only where they: (1) are pending trial, or on probation, or under court supervision at the time of their arrest; (2) pose a significant flight risk; or (3) present an articulable danger to a particular person or the community in general. That is it. Many newly-elected progressive prosecutors are still struggling to enact laws as liberal as those in D.C. If I'd been arrested in D.C., I could rest assured that I would not be detained pre-trial, assuming I had even been charged. But I wasn't in D.C.; I was in Manhattan.

But all was not lost. I knew that at some point, before any charge would be officially filed against me, the Arresting Officer would have an opportunity to confer with the Manhattan DA's office. He would speak to the on-duty or intake prosecutor tasked with making preliminary charging decisions. The Assistant District Attorney (ADA) would ask the Arresting Officer to relay what happened, and he would give his side of the story. The ADA might even ask the officer for his opinion on whether to charge me. But it was ultimately up to the ADA to decide whether and with what to charge. All I could do was hope that the ADA screener was like Rosie.

Rosie was a career prosecutor at the U.S. Attorney's Office in D.C. She largely handled pre-litigation Domestic Violence misdemeanor and felony cases. She reviewed, signed, and declined warrants, and for years, she handled most of the domestic violence screening or intake of cases. Rosie was famous in our office for not papering nonsense. In other words, over the years, she developed a knack for distinguishing the good cases from the bad, the "victims," that were not inclined to be cooperative, and the defendants who deserved another chance to avoid having a record.

As a misdemeanor AUSA in the domestic violence (DV) intake unit, it was a privilege to "pick up" or receive case assignments when Rosie was screening. It was equally as desirable to be a part of the intake team when Rosie was in the lead-intake chair. When I began prosecuting felony domestic violence cases, I was flattered to learn that some officers referred to me as "*little Rosie*", due to my efficiency and, if I'm totally honest, my sass.

And so, I prayed.

Ok, God. Please let the screener be Black; please let her be like Rosie; please let her see this case for exactly what it is—a case of driving while Black. Please let her consider the totality of circumstances, the gray—the way Rosie would. God, please let this case be "no papered." Amen.

CHAPTER 6: "YOU'RE NOT AN ATTORNEY!"

In the blink of an eye, everything changes. One minute, you're at a comedy club, looking forward to comfortably falling asleep in a downtown Marriott bed; the next, you're in handcuffs, in the back of a squad car, trying to understand how the night could have gone so far off course.

It was the night after Thanksgiving. For weeks, Joseph and I had planned to go to New York for the holiday. There, at my mother's home in Baldwin, Long Island, our families would meet for the first time. For weeks, we had planned to see his brother, a financier by day and a comedian by night, perform stand-up at Broadway Comedy club.

A few days before the show, we decided to book a hotel in lower Manhattan to avoid the late-night drive back to Long Island. The show started around 8 p.m. and ended around 11 p.m. There were some decent comedians, but no one worth the price that we ultimately paid for a night out in the big city. After the show, we stopped for gas near West 40th Street, in a section of the city known as "Hell's Kitchen". We filled up, and started heading toward the West Side Highway, expecting to be downtown in a matter of minutes—traffic permitting. A few blocks later, we were flagged down, and directed to pull over by the police.

A moderately built brown-skinned officer approached our car. He appeared to be in training that day—I'll call him the "Rookie." The Rookie approached the driver's side of the car and began to engage with Joseph. "Hi, do you know why I'm stopping you?" "No," Joseph responded, an honest answer. We definitely weren't speeding. "I'm stopping you because you failed to use your turn signal at that light." He then asked Joseph for his license and registration.

I noticed that there were several other officers standing around, and that we were not the only cars stopped. It appeared that everyone who made that left turn toward the highway had been pulled over, but we were the only ones detained. I noticed the car immediately in front of us, operated by a white driver, was immediately allowed to pull off without so much as providing documents. I expected the Rookie to hand Joseph his driver's license and send us on our way. It was late. I was tired. It was my last night with Joseph before a weeklong trip; I wanted to have a peaceful night. But our police encounter was far from over.

Within seconds of asking Joseph for his documents, the Rookie requested that Joseph step out of the car. Before that moment, I was not paying much attention to the Rookie, or to his exchange with Joseph; but with that one request—"sir, please put the car in park and step out of the vehicle"—the Rookie now had my undivided attention. We were a young black couple, casually dressed, late on a Friday night. We were driving a 2020 Camaro, with semi-tinted windows. Joseph, tall, dark and sizeable, was wearing a red hoodie at the time of the stop. I suspected that we had been profiled. Not only did I live in New York City at the height of the debate on New York's "stop and frisk" program, I'd spent the last few years watching this exact scenario play itself out on body-worn camera as an AUSA. I knew exactly what was up.

As a prosecutor, you learn that your voice, your judgment,

and your sense of fairness are your most important assets. Speaking up in the midst of misconduct was a part of the job; it was something I could not easily turn off, especially when it came down to the interests of someone I loved. So I decided to speak up: "*Why is he being asked to step out of the car? That [white] person wasn't asked to step out of the car! Why is he being asked to step out of the car?*" I reached for the only piece of identification I had to show that I am a lawyer — my DOJ identification card. "*Perhaps if the officer knows that I'm an attorney, he will keep the foolishness to a minimum*," I thought. I was wrong. The Rookie refused to look at it. "Put that away," he said, or words to that effect. I got the impression he noticed the DOJ seal and assumed I was a federal agent trying to pull rank on his local law enforcement authority.

Then the patronizing rhetoric began: "In New York, once I have probable cause to stop the car, I can ask any occupant to step out," he said, adding condescendingly, "Maybe you don't know the law . . . Google it." I was, in fact, very familiar with the law. I was familiar with the fact that the Rookie was selectively enforcing it. Of course he could request that occupants step out of the car, but he was not permitted to do so on the basis of race or any other protected characteristic. Notwithstanding my protests, it was clear that the Rookie was committed to removing Joseph from the car. Nothing I could say was going to change that. At a loss for options, Joseph looked at me and I looked back at him feeling powerless. He opened the driver's side door and stepped outside.

I waited, initially. I waited for enough time to pass for the Rookie to issue Joseph a ticket; after all, we had been stopped for failing to use a turn signal, allegedly. I waited until waiting felt too passive to be justifiable. Unable to see or hear what was happening outside of the car from the inside, I stepped out and tried to record the encounter.

Joseph, whose back was towards me, heard the officer address me. Realizing that I was outside of the car, Joseph looked over to me and said, "They're telling me I either have to take a Breathalyzer or go to jail." The Rookie interrupted, "I'm not *telling* you anything; don't put words in my mouth, I'm asking you." *Right*—a distinction without a difference.

The reality is that there is no such thing as "asking" when it comes to police officer encounters. A refusal to comply with any request easily becomes a disobeyed order used to justify an arrest. Indeed, these officers had already told Joseph that if he refused the Breathalyzer, the consequence would be jail. I could see the worry on Joseph's face. There were now multiple officers taking an interest in our traffic stop after having let their "less suspicious" travelers go.

Instinctively, I started to walk toward Joseph. It happened naturally after sensing his discomfort; but the Arresting Officer charged at me anyway. I re-entered the car, but not before letting Joseph know that he was perfectly within his right not to blow. At some point I would be asked by a senior DOJ official, "Why not just stay in the car and let the traffic stop play itself out?" In other words, why not accept that these types of police contacts are inherent to being Black. After all, even the Supreme Court has deemed itself "powerless"[i] against these sorts of intrusions. In the weeks and months following my arrest, I became utterly sick and tired of those who would not find themselves in my situation—not even on their worst day—telling me how I should have responded.

The officers had resorted to scare tactics. Both the Rookie and the Arresting Officer were telling Joseph that, if he did not blow, he would be arrested, and his license would be suspended. I called out to him from inside of the car, "*Your license will be suspended in New York; you don't live here, it doesn't fucking matter!*" That was the truth. Several administrative steps are required before the licensing jurisdiction learns of an offense resulting in suspension or revocation in another state. It was highly probable that Joseph's right to drive in New York could be suspended without it ever having any impact on his ability to drive in Washington, D.C., or any neighboring state. Still, neither officer took kindly to me advising Joseph, as they tried to cow him into submission. "She doesn't know what she's talking about," they said, pompously.

I continued to wait. I waited until my waiting felt like abandonment. I could not help but wonder what else they were saying to him. I am an advocate, at my core. How could I sit back and not advocate for him? And what if this goes bad? What if they draw weapons? *I will not be the next Diamond Reynolds.* And, with that thought, I exited the car. I did what I had been trained to do, what I was born to do, I advocated: "*At this point, I am his attorney and he's not saying anything else!*"

The Arresting Officer looked at me and said:

"*You're not an attorney!*"

Whoa. I was stunned. His words spoke volumes. Why was it so hard for him to believe that this casually dressed Black girl had a J.D.? "I am an attorney!" I exclaimed. "No you're not," he retorted back. "I'm an attorney, I'm barred in New York, and he's not saying shit else." Within seconds, the Arresting Officer had me pressed up against the car, hands behind my back, and handcuffed. He told me that I was being placed under arrest for OGA, an acronym I would not understand for another few hours. He added that he was going to "top [me] off" with resisting arrest despite the fact that I had not resisted in any way whatsoever.

As he escorted me to the squad car, he commented to his fellow officers, "She keeps saying she's an attorney." This man would continue to question whether I was an attorney, even after he searched my bag and read my DOJ identification card with his own eyes.

It still baffles me that the Arresting Officer found it so hard to believe that I could be a lawyer. At this point in my life, the novelty of my law degree has worn off. What wakes me up in the morning is not that piece of paper, or my title. What gets my adrenaline going is being a voice for the voiceless; using my talent to do, solely, what I believe to be right. I have no loyalty to any party, administration, attorney general, supervisor, or policy; my only allegiance is to justice, and that is a rare and personally rewarding space to occupy. I say that to say, the Arresting Officer's utter inability to conceive that I could be an attorney did not offend my pride, it offended my sense of fairness.

His small-mindedness revealed his bias—a bias that consistently ravages our communities. At its best, this bias permits citizen-harassment, the type of harassment that Joseph and I experienced on that November night. At its worst, this bias takes lives. The Arresting Officer's bias is reflected in policies implemented throughout the country that encourage the disproportionate and over-aggressive targeting of poor and Black communities; his bias was no different from that which led a Minnesota officer to shoot and kill Philando Castile in the presence of his partner and 4-year old child; or that which resulted in the killings of Atatiana Jefferson and Botham Jean in their respective homes. It is the same bias that led a Minneapolis officer to kneel mercilessly on George Floyd's neck as he begged for reprieve; the same bias that took the lives of Breonna Taylor in Kentucky, Trayvon Martin in Florida, Elijah McClain in Colorado, Freddie Gray in Baltimore, Oscar Grant in California, and countless other Black and brown, male and female bodies, senselessly killed by men and women sworn to protect; Bias that is completely incompatible with keeping Black bodies safe when they are predominantly viewed as the public enemy.

So, there I was . . . handcuffed, in a squad car, and on my way to jail. These officers could have given me a desk appearance ticket or citation with a date to appear in court, but they did not think enough of my liberty to do so. In fact, they thought so little of my life that they forgot to fasten my seatbelt before we started making our way toward the precinct. Late the next day, after my release, I realized for the first time, that the Arresting Officer's physical handling of me had left a scar on my lower back—a four to five inch, vertical laceration that would serve as a vivid reminder of our interaction each time I walked by a full-length mirror.

As I rode in that squad car, I gave some thought to crying and begging apologetically for my release—showing a little humility and remorse for insulting the officers' pride. I knew that might score some good will with these power-tripping, egomaniacs, but I couldn't bring myself to do it. I wouldn't give them the satisfaction. I refused to shrink so that they could feel strong. Ultimately, I knew that, while these officers held the cards in that moment, they would not have the final word. Knowing that helped me survive the embarrassment, the assault on my good name, my character, and my ethics, in addition to the fear that those with the power to derail my career, actually would.

One of the last times that I saw the Arresting Officer was during his gratuitous visit to my cell. I had watched him rummage through my purse, hoping to find something good, something criminal. I had watched him use my DOJ credential to complete his police paperwork; to support the false accusation that I verbally identified myself as an AUSA, while he and his comrades unlawfully detained Joseph and me on a public road.

At my cell, he would tell me that I was charged with "OGA."

I'd ask what that meant, and he would yell, "How can you be an attorney and not know what OGA means?" I responded, indignantly, "I don't practice here [*you idiot*]. We probably call it something else in D.C." It was clear that even after seeing my title with his own eyes, it was still difficult for him to see me as a lawyer. That visit to my cell would be his final opportunity to flex his power, to let me know that he was in charge. He advised me that Joseph "blew a .03" and was not arrested. He added "You two could be with each other in your own bed, if it wasn't for your mouth."

And there it was. I had not been arrested for obstructing governmental administration or resisting arrest. Those were just fancy statutory phrases that empowered him to lock me in a cage. I had been arrested for getting under his skin, for speaking too boldly. As written by the late Maya Angelou, my sassiness had upset him, my haughtiness had offended him; he wanted to see me broken, bowed head and lowered eyes. But there was no way I would give him that satisfaction.

I was not going to beg for his mercy . . . not in the squad car, not ever. He would soon learn that just like air, I was certain to rise.

CHAPTER 7: THE OTHER SIDE OF THE "V."

Around 7:00 a.m., an officer opened our cell door. It was the Transport Officer, the nicer one. He told us that it was time to head to central booking, where we would see a judge. He then cuffed us and walked us out of the precinct, where the Arresting Officer waited for us in a transport vehicle.

I was still angry with the Arresting Officer, but I knew I had to play the long game. I knew he would have a chance to weigh in on what should happen with my case. At some point, an ADA would contact him, given his role, to get his perspective. During that call or in-person meeting, he would have the ability to say, "*You know what, let's just let it go. Yeah, she got under my skin, but one night in jail is probably enough.*" While the ADA would ultimately make the final decision, she could very well take his opinion into account; after all, it is the prosecutor who decides—among other things—who, whether, and what to charge through the exercise of "prosecutorial discretion."

The exercise of "prosecutorial discretion" is the core of the prosecutorial function. It can only be described as an amazing power; an outcome-determinative power; a power often and rightly criticized as largely unchecked. In addition to deciding who, whether, and what to charge, the prosecutor's initial evaluation of a case impacts the liberty restraint imposed on the accused. While the law defines the circumstances that allow for pre-trial detention, the prosecutor decides whether to request that such detention be imposed. If the prosecutor finds a basis to seek dismissal of a case – even as late as the day of trial, she is under no obligation to explain her decision to the defense or to the judge. She simply moves to dismiss, a motion the judge is unlikely to deny, and the defense is unlikely to oppose.

I once sought dismissal of a case on the day of trial, after coming across a video that substantially undermined the officer's initial report. I was required to obtain internal approval to dismiss, which my supervisors gave not out of concern for the rights of the accused; but to protect the officer, who would have been demolished on the stand by the defense, and potentially deemed incredible by a judge. After dismissal was granted, the judge called me to the bench to ask what, if any, information I could give him to explain my dismissal request. I had been expressly told by supervisors to say, "prosecutorial discretion." I did what I was told, and the discussion ended there. I did not realize then that an entire body of case law exists to shield prosecutorial decision-making from public scrutiny. And so, while I knew that what happened next with *my case* was up to the ADA, I figured playing nice with the Arresting Officer would not hurt.

I noticed that he was also playing nice. He was speaking to me kindly. He was smiling. He was gentle as he helped me into and out of the transport vehicle. This time, he remembered to fasten my seatbelt. When the trip ended, he told me, "Perhaps we'll meet again under different circumstances." It made me cringe to play this game, but I hoped it would result in a "no paper," as we call it in D.C. There, "no paper" means that the prosecution has used its discretion to decline to file charges. But, as you know, that is not how the story went.

Perhaps the Arresting Officer did advocate in favor of a "no paper" in my case, and the intake ADA disagreed. Maybe the Arresting Officer leaked my story to the N.Y. Post, thereby forcing the ADA's hand. I may never know. Eventually, our trip came to an end. That would be the last time I laid eyes on the Arresting Officer in person.

Once out of the car, the Transport Officer escorted Isis and me through central booking where more handling and processing awaited us. It seemed as though we were the first "lock-ups" there. The Transport Officer observed that the courthouse was unusually empty, and suggested we might be released before lunch. His optimism filled us with expectation and hope. In reality, we had at least another twelve hours to go. Perhaps he, too, was handling us, but because he was a decent human being, I'll give him the benefit of the doubt.

Soon I would learn that the Processing Officer was either misinformed, or gaslighting me. I had been charged with a misdemeanor, not a felony. I would not be held beyond my initial appearance. There would be no request for bail. I would be released on my own personal promise to return to court at a later date—that is, of course, if the DA actually charged me. I would spend the next several hours praying for a declination. By 1:00 p.m. or so, I spoke with my attorney, Lance Clarke, for the first time. He confirmed that the DA would be moving forward with a case against me. *The People of the State of New York v. Bianca Forde* was a foregone conclusion. I was now officially on the other side of the "v."

CHAPTER 8: THE WAIT AIN'T OVER

The Transport Officer had given us false hope by suggesting we would be released by late morning. "This place is usually packed," he said. "You'll definitely see a judge soon," he added. There it was again, that relative term - "soon." I suppose one's interpretation of the word will vary according to their circumstances. As I approached hour eight in custody, "soon" would never be soon enough. The term euphemistically suggested that our wait was almost over when there was much more waiting, and even more processing to come.

We were required to undergo a health assessment, if one could even call it that. We were taken to a room where we were asked a series of questions. For the woman asking them, it was clear that the process had become rote: "Are you on any medication?" I had been in custody for eight hours, and this was the first time anyone had asked me if I needed meds. Thank God, the answer was no.

The questions continued. "Have you been treated for HIV, hepatitis, high blood pressure? Have you considered suicide?" I paused. "Maybe just today," I responded, mostly in jest. I retracted the statement almost immediately to avoid triggering the need for any additional reports or paperwork, which would most certainly add to my processing time. But my interviewer did not skip a beat. She was as eager to dismiss my suicidal ideations as sarcasm as I was. Was I joking? Maybe. Did I understand how someone in the same situation might not be? Absolutely.

An hour or so after my release, as I was stepping into the shower to wash eighteen hours of jail-filth off of my person, I would speak with my cousin Renee by phone. Renee is a wife, and mother of two Black boys. Renee and her sister Natalie were both like sisters to me growing up. The three of us attended the same elementary, middle, and high schools, largely at the same time. When each school day ended, we would commune under the care of Grandma Lucille, until she passed in 1998.

Renee, bless her heart, is a crier; so it did not surprise me when she burst into tears upon hearing my voice over the phone. I realized that she was expressing emotions that I had not yet acknowledged, but soon would. Her tears conveyed both a sense of relief that I was home and safe, as well as terror about what could have been. A few days later, after returning to D.C., I visited Renee in Maryland. There, she had a chance to explain to me just how terrified she was upon learning that I had been arrested, was in jail, and that no one in the family had any information on where I was or how long I would be there.

After my arrest, I did not call my family to let them know what happened. I foolishly thought I could keep the incident to myself, aside from my disclosure obligations with respect to the DOJ. However, the reporters had not only started calling my job; they had started calling my family. Renee tried to reach me and Joseph—who was under strict orders from me not to tell *anyone* what had happened. Renee's inability to reach us made her more frightened. Absent assurances that I was ok, she explained that her mind centered on Sandra Bland.

As I watched tears stream down her face, I could not help but recall the similarities between my story and that of Sandra Bland. Like Joseph and me, Ms. Bland's contact with the criminal justice system began as a traffic stop. Like us, she'd been pulled over for failing to use a turn signal. After what the media described as a "confrontational traffic stop,"[i] Ms. Bland was taken into custody and held for three days. Yes, three days; seventy-two hours. On the third day, Ms. Bland was found hanging in her cell, and medical professionals deemed it a suicide.[ii] The third day? How could this be, when the Supreme Court has deemed any period of post-arrest detention above forty-eight hours presumptively unreasonable.

I remembered how N.Y.C. central booking personnel informed us that we could be held for up to seventy-two hours. I did not know then, and do not know now, what legal precedent they were relying upon to maintain or announce that policy. After spending just eighteen hours in jail, the thought of seventy-two was, and is, unfathomable. So, no, I had not considered suicide; but I most certainly understood how someone could.

After the "health exam" ended, there was one more round of questioning. The Transport Officer took us down a stairwell and into a room occupied by two guards. A correctional officer, with a strong Haitian accent, would be one of our guards for the next several hours. For a moment, I wished I had learned a few words of Haitian Creole from Joseph—anything that would earn me a bit of grace with someone in a position to grant it. The Correctional Officer administered the final round of questioning, a prerequisite for the final round of waiting. These questions included a series of physical health questions, the most memorable of which was whether I was pregnant. Eight hours in custody, and someone had just now thought it fit to ask whether

I was carrying precious cargo.

Next, the Correctional Officer needed to search me. I had been thoroughly searched at the precinct, and had not been in contact with anyone except law enforcement and Isis (who had also been searched) since my arrest; but, I suppose, anything is possible. The officer took everything out of my pockets, inclusive of only a tissue and a few dollars. She requested that I let my hair down and took away my hairpins. She ran her gloved hands through my hair to check for contraband. She returned my tissue and dollar bills but kept my hairpins. The prior day's wash-and-go, coupled with a night in a jail cell, did not bode well for this *naturalista*! The last thing I needed was to appear unkempt before a judge. I did not yet know that the judge would be the least of my concerns, given the courtroom press.

After the search, I was taken to another cell. It was the second-to-last holding cell I would occupy that day. It was easily four times the size of the cell Isis and I shared, which was necessary since we were no longer a twosome. We shared this new cell with several other bodies — the stoic, seemingly *built-for-this-life* type. I arrived first; it seemed like forever before Isis joined me.

While I waited, longingly, for her familiar face, I assessed my new surroundings, being careful not to look any one person in the eye, or for too long. I channeled my New York City Subway rider persona, and I minded my own business. I sat on the bench closest to the egress point of the cell, still in disbelief of the calculations that I was now required to make. I calmed myself the way I often do on roller coasters, centering my mind on the fact that *this would not be the way God planned to take me out.* I put my head down, I prayed, and I waited. That was all I could do.

Most of my new cellmates were on benches, others on the floor. These benches were painted black and were half the size of the bench that Isis and I shared at the precinct. One false move while laying on them, and you would easily fall flat on your face onto the floor. I suspect that's why so many opted to skip a step and lay on the filthy holding cell tile. Who was I to judge? God knows how long they'd been there, given New York's dubious seventy-two-hour rule.

I racked my brain, trying to understand the basis of this 72-hour rule. In D.C., we recognize the Supreme Court's 48-hour dictate as the upper boundary of reasonableness for post-arrest detention; however, we strive to ensure that a judge sees all arrestees, and rules on release or detention, within 24 hours of the arrest. Either New York City was blatantly ignoring Supreme Court precedent, or deliberately playing mind games with those in custody. I had plenty of time to ponder this and other matters as I waited for Isis to enter this new, communal cell.

Isis was young and green, but equally as kind and endearing. I waited patiently for her to finish the final round of processing, and enter our new holding place. Hours later, I'd refer to her as my jailbird sister, when she gave me her extra elastic hair tie, sparing me from looking too disheveled in those newspaper photos. At some point that day, I thought we might end up staying in touch. By the time we parted ways, I realized that whatever comfort we offered each other during that limited period was part of an experience we simply preferred to leave behind.

Finally, the cell door opened, and there she was. There was no open space next to me, so she sat on an adjacent bench in between two other women. We bided our time, doing our best to fly under the radar while assessing the new cast of characters.

CHAPTER 9: WHITE PRIVILEGE IN LIVING COLOR

The diversity of my cellmates was striking to me. It was markedly different from the seamless stream of Black and brown faces that flowed in lockstep through D.C. Superior Court, and the U.S. District Court for the District of Columbia (hereinafter, "Federal Court").

First, there was Angela, a Spanish-speaker, who I suspected was as unfamiliar with the inside of a N.Y.C. jail cell as Isis and me. Next to her was a woman who may have been Latina or Asian. She never spoke, and I never learned her name. At some point, after finally falling asleep, I woke up from a nap, and she was gone.

Laid out next to me was a twenty-something Asian woman I'll call Lynn. Lynn had been arrested for switching tags on clothing in Century-21, a department store in lower Manhattan. Security observed her switching the tags, and before she could pay, she was detained. Before her release, I learned that her husband was arrested with her, presumably for the same type of offense.

To my far right was a heavyset young, white woman. She was likely in her late-twenties or early-thirties. She was comfortably asleep when I arrived, or so it appeared; although I could not figure out how, since half of her body was spilling over the bench. She wore a very stylish camouflage denim jacket. It was tapered in the waist, giving the illusion of an appealing waist-to-hip ratio. We'll call her Brenda.

I later learned that Brenda had been arrested for driving under the influence (DUI). She was the backseat passenger of a tinted Yukon stopped for suspicion of DUI. Her boyfriend was driving, and a friend occupied the front passenger seat. All were intoxicated. However, since the driver and passenger had prior DUI convictions, Brenda agreed to assume the role of driver once they were stopped, but before the police approached the vehicle. Apparently, she knew that if charged with a DUI, she would face probation only, while the other occupants would likely receive jail time.

I found it shocking that the officers did not notice any suspicious motion upon approaching the car. Certainly, they must have seen the shadows of bodies moving as their lights flashed into the vehicle, or observed actual movement of the SUV given what would be required for multiple occupants to change positions in this way. They must have seen something that would at least trigger an inquiry, right? After all, I have reviewed countless police reports prepared by officers who cite to "furtive gestures" or sudden movements as their basis to search or detain occupants. These cases, more often than not, involve young Black men, however; and Brenda and her friends were young and White. In any event, I listened to Brenda tell her story, and wondered why she would willingly put herself in a position to be charged and convicted of DUI when she was not the driver. I suppose she was aware that one DUI would do nothing to tarnish her privilege.

Toward the back of the cell, immediately across from the cell door entrance, were four women I'll call Maria, Kim, Nikki, and Marlene. Maria was asleep when I arrived. She remained asleep until her case was called. I envied her, the same way I envied Isis.

Nothing would make the time pass faster than being able to fall asleep.

Surrounding Maria on separate benches were Kim, Nikki, and Marlene. Kim was asleep on the floor when I entered the cell, but I never learned why she was in custody. She had the junkie lean, so I assumed her arrest had something to do with drugs.

Nikki was passed out in a seated position on the bench farthest from the locked cell door. She was one of the first to see the judge. She had been arrested for shoplifting, but was sure to announce that she had previously beaten a murder charge before exiting the cell.

Marlene lay prone and asleep on a middle bench when I first arrived. She left shortly after Nikki, but not before offering the group sound advice: "Never keep your jail clothes," she cautioned us, "They're bad luck." She added, "I love this hoodie, but I'm burning it as soon as I get out. The only thing I'm keeping is my coat." *Wise words?* Perhaps. Marlene's theory was that jail clothes had bad juju, and keeping them would lead to more legal troubles. I briefly considered discarding the new, quilted, crop-top sweater I was wearing at the time, but opted against it. Based on her statements, I surmised Marlene was no first-time offender. I thought it unlikely that her clothes were the reason she had found herself in DOC custody time and time again. With that thought, I decided my sweater would live to see another day.

Toward the middle of the afternoon, Colleen arrived. She had a heavy Irish accent, and had been arrested following a Domestic Violence (DV) incident. She and her boyfriend had a fistfight, and he had called 911. He later apologized, admitting that he did not realize that Colleen would be arrested on sight.

In many jurisdictions, officers are legally required to detain the aggressor in a DV dispute. The law is aimed at ensuring that once the police leave, the aggressor does not cause additional harm to the victim. Many folks don't realize that. So, they call the police to intervene, and then become angry when the police do their jobs. But Colleen had a bigger problem. She had recently migrated to the U.S., and held only a green card. This arrest could impact her legal status in the U.S.

As I listened to Colleen describe her predicament, I could not help but reflect on the racial and ethnic diversity of the women with whom I shared a jail cell. Certainly, New York City was leading the charge for diversity and inclusion in lock-ups.

One of the last to arrive at the jail that day, and the very last to leave—was Kerry-Ann. A tall, white woman I disliked almost instantly. She spoke with a confidence that far surpassed the value she added to the world, and casually used the word "nigga" in conversation in a way that infuriated me. It took significant restraint for me not to call her out for doing so; but I decided I did not need another battle, especially a battle with someone who had far less to lose than I did.

One of the many things I learned about Kerry-Ann that day was that she'd been arrested on suspicion of DUI. It's called "suspicion of" because (unlike Brenda) Kerry-Ann had refused to blow into the Breathalyzer—the smart choice without question. As much as it sucks to be arrested, suspicion of DUI is far better than blowing, and thus providing the scientific evidence needed to confirm the suspicion.

Kerry-Ann bragged about how she'd expressed her rage at the officers on scene — yelling, cursing, and calling them names. I expected that maybe, she too, had been charged at, pushed against a car, and "topped off" with resisting. Instead, she described how the officers apologized to her, expressing regret for having to arrest her. I listened to her gloat, and could not understand how this basic and belligerent White girl was deemed deserving of an apology. Her pugnacious behavior, now directed at the DOC guards, continued throughout the day without consequence — white privilege at its finest. *Must be nice.*

CHAPTER 10: PAPARAZZI'S GONNA GET YA!

Joseph's phone had seemingly died or something. This man, who never misses any of my calls, had chosen this moment to miss about a dozen of them. I had no idea what was going on, but it certainly did not ease my anxiety. I had called him repeatedly from the precinct, and I had no idea when I would have access to another phone once we left for central booking. I had been in the central booking holding cell for about an hour before I realized that there was a payphone affixed to the wall. I was not certain it would work, but I decided to test it out.

As I stood up and walked toward the phone, all eyes were on me. It seemed the others had also failed to notice the pay phone, or had simply assumed that it was non-functioning wall décor. As I dialed "1-800 collect", everyone waited to see whether an outgoing call would be successful. It took a few tries, but it worked, and in that moment, Joseph's voice was the most reassuring sound I had ever heard. I immediately felt a sense of relief. I knew I was not alone.

I could hear the emotion in his voice—the fear, the regret, the helplessness. Apparently, he'd gone to his brother's home in Harlem to wait for my release, and the reception there was sub-optimal. One week later, I would watch the body-worn camera footage related to the incident, and I could almost see Joseph's heart break as the Arresting Officer put me in cuffs. Joseph pleaded with them not to take me away but to no avail. He has never been able to watch the body camera footage.

The last thing I said to Joseph, as I was being placed in the squad car, was "Call Bryan." Bryan had become a brother to me. At the time, we were both prosecutors at the United States Attorney's Office–DC (USAO–DC). Bryan had also spent a number of years at the Manhattan DA's office. I needed a lawyer, and I knew that I could trust Bryan for a quality recommendation. *"Call Bryan, tell him what happened, but don't tell him it's me."* Those were my instructions.

Joseph followed those instructions, at least initially. Bryan recommended Lance A. Clarke. It happened to be Lance's birthday. Lance had a number of other client-business to handle that day, followed by a birthday party with his family and some of his closest friends. He was on a schedule, and I was not an expected part of it. Lance was fitting me in, but not as fast as Joseph would have liked. So Joseph spilled the beans. In tears, he explained to Bryan that he had not been calling about a random friend; he was calling about me. Things seemed to forge forward at that point. Lance contacted the Manhattan DA, but it was a bit too late. Someone had leaked the story of my arrest. A decision to decline my case would communicate a dangerous message of entitlement and a lack of accountability. They had to charge me. One prosecutor's career is a small price to pay to preserve optics.

Still, I was grateful to Lance for trying. I was even more grateful to him for delaying his birthday dinner to get me out of jail. Lance knew that if I had paid counsel, I'd be released sooner. The public defenders remain in the courtroom as needed; the clients of paid attorneys get priority. Lance may have spared me another several hours in a holding cell, and for that, I owe him a debt of gratitude. We spoke several times that day over the cellblock payphone. He confirmed that he'd get to the courthouse around 6:30 p.m. Finally, there was an end in sight.

Until then, our holding cell payphone would be in heavy rotation. Once the other ladies knew that the phone worked, everyone realized they had at least one person they could call. When we were not speaking to loved ones on the other side of the bars, we spoke to one another; we sat; we talked; we told stories; we even laughed. We laughed at Isis and her youthful naivety. We joked about Kerry-Ann's oblivious co-workers, who thought it appropriate to tell their boss that Kerry-Ann had been arrested. We chuckled about Colleen's boyfriend, who retained paid counsel on her behalf, believing that made up for him calling the police. He had no idea what was in store for him when she returned home. In those moments of laughter, we temporarily forgot where we were. I gained a new and profound understanding of the idiom, "laughter is the best medicine."

I called Joseph once every thirty-minutes for updates—$250 worth of collect calls, according to his December mobile phone bill. Whatever he learned from the courtroom staff about timing, he shared with me, and I shared with my new, temporary friends. We were all so different, but while sharing that cell, we were on the same side, literally and figuratively. Soon, names would be called to see the judge. Guards would come to the cell to collect our "bodies" for presentment. Kerry-Ann and I would be the last to leave. She was my least favorite of the crew, so I did not waste time making small talk with her while I waited for my name to be called. We waited in silence. Finally, I heard a guard say "Forde". I stood up and walked swiftly to the cell door as if I feared she might change her mind. The door opened, and I said goodbye to Kerry-Ann. Served her right to be last for being such a bitch.

The female guard handed me off to a male guard, who

handed me off to another. All chatted amongst themselves, never so much as saying hello to me or acknowledging that I was there. I was simply a body that they had to get from point A to point B. Indeed, in courtrooms in Washington, D.C., it was not unusual to hear prosecutors, judges, court staff, and even the defense, use the term "body" to describe the accused's escorted movement throughout the courthouse. Thus, I knew exactly what I was to those guards—a body; nothing more, nothing less.

Eventually, I was taken to the final holding area—an area behind the courtroom where the judge was sitting. Brenda, Isis, and Lynn were all still there waiting. Lynn was in a little booth, speaking with her attorney. Isis told me that someone called my name a few minutes before I walked in. I knew it must have been Lance. I walked toward the cellblock door to tell the guard my lawyer may have called out for me already. This one actually looked me in my eye and responded: "It's ok," he said, "your lawyer will be back to check for you again." A small but powerful act of humanity.

He was right. Lance came back a few minutes later. I started to sit inside of the booth to tell my story, but Lance stopped me. "We'll talk later," he said. "I'll let them know you're here so we can call the case." He walked back out, and I sat down next to Isis. When my name was called, I said goodbye to my jailhouse sister and wished her luck.

The guard came for me shortly thereafter and escorted me into the courtroom, to an area reserved for the "lock-ups" or arrestees. We had similar areas in D.C. criminal courtrooms, of course; but I'd never so much as even walked across those spaces. Rather, I'd stand at the table or podium reserved for the representative of the United States, awaiting the accused's arrival into the courtroom. When handling presentments, the accused's first appearance in a criminal case, I would survey him, his demeanor, his respect or lack thereof for the process. I suspected that others were now surveying me in the same way. For the first time in my life, I'd entered a courtroom not as counsel, or even as a student, but as the accused.

As I waited for my case to be called, I sat on a bench next to Lynn and Brenda, now observing the courtroom from this new vantage point. I watched Lance interact with the prosecution and the courtroom staff. I could tell that he was well-liked and respected—all signs of a promising pick. Minutes later, my case was called; *People of New York v. Bianca Forde.* I started to stand, but both Lance and the bailiff instructed me to wait. I sat back down. "*Strange,*" I thought. Lance started to speak, and I listened.

Apparently, the courtroom was filled with press. I had not noticed. They were all there, waiting like vultures to photograph the federal prosecutor arrested in a "drunk driving incident," as the headlines misleadingly read. Lance petitioned the court for the exclusion of the press. He argued that, as a federal prosecutor, having my name and photograph in the paper posed a safety risk. Brenda and Lynn looked at me, stunned. They didn't speak, but it was clear what they were thinking: "*What, you're a Fed?!*"

The judge appeared to consider Lance's request for as long as it would take to blink an eye. "*Denied,*" he said, completely devoid of any compassion. Instantly, the paparazzi flooded the front of the courtroom, and the bailiff directed me to take my rightful, yet unfamiliar, position beside Lance. As I approached the podium, the cameras began to flicker uncontrollably. All of this, for me? I had never seen anything like it. We do not allow cameras in D.C. courtrooms—not even for high-profile prosecutions of presidential political allies.

When it was over, the cameras followed us out of the courtroom. Luckily, I was wearing a hooded coat that could hide my face. Joseph walked out in front of me, shielding me as best as he could. I knew how badly he wanted to smash those reporters' prized cameras. Had he done so, I would not have blamed him.

Lance walked out behind us. He shook Joseph's hand and gave me a hug. He assured me, as he would do every time we spoke for the next several months, that everything would be okay. "Small things to a giant," he would often say—an effective reminder of who I was, what I stood for, and that this too would pass. Prior to that day, I had not met nor heard of Lance A. Clarke. I had not had the opportunity to research him, and I did not need to. He was my lawyer, and with time, he would become my friend.

With Lance and the cameras now gone, Joseph opened the car door for me, and we both entered the car. For the first time in eighteen hours, I was safe. For the first time in eighteen hours, my needs mattered. For the first time in eighteen hours, I was human, and I would be treated as such. For the first time in eighteen hours, I could show weakness; I could be vulnerable. It was now safe to let everything out that I was feeling. If I had recorded myself, there's a good chance I let out an Isis-*ish* wail. Joseph held me. He kissed me. He assured me that we were in this together, and that it would all be okay.

CHAPTER 11: ARREST 101

When you are arrested, no one hands you a roadmap, or gives you a sense of what to expect. I suppose, if they did, it would read something like this:

Good evening, Ms. Forde. Thank you for joining us. The officer, who saw fit to arrest you, has some paperwork to complete. Accordingly, you will sit here, in this cell, until he is finished. It will take a significant amount of time. We are not sure why, because it really is not that complicated, especially for a case such as yours, but we like to take our time.

Once your paperwork is in, there are a few administrative steps that require your participation. We will have to enter your fingerprints into our system, where they will forever be. That way, if you ever even think about committing another crime, especially a violent one, perhaps you'll think twice. We will also need to capture your mugshot for our law enforcement databases. If you're lucky, it won't end up on Google.

Eventually, we will take you to central booking, located at the courthouse, where you will ultimately appear before a judge. I say "ultimately" because we like to let our arrestees know that you may be waiting to see a judge for up to seventy-two hours. Yes, the Supreme Court presumes anything over forty-eight hours is unreasonable, but this is New York, and we like to mess with your head.

Once you get to central booking, there are additional administrative steps we have to take. More fingerprinting, more photos – including photos of your irises. We will ask you questions about your mental and physical health, not because we care about your wellbeing, but to protect ourselves against liability, you know—like what happened with that woman, Sandra Bland. We do the bare minimum to ensure that you don't die on our watch. We can't afford any more lawsuits.

Once we have determined that you are not a liability, and will not require special care, you will be placed in another holding cell. This one will be larger and have more occupants. You'll interact with dozens of women throughout the day. You will all wait to see a judge, but do not fret. We will try to ensure that nonviolent and violent offenders do not commingle.

While you wait, there will be guards, but the last thing they will want to do is talk to you. They will come by every few hours with food because they are required to. But they will be loathed to answer your questions. Don't ask them for updates; it will get you nowhere.

You and the other women in your cell will share a toilet. You will have to hold the door while you squat to take care of your business. There will be no privacy. You will all hear and smell everything that happens in that stall so, if you can, avoid the food that is offered to you.

There will be a payphone in this cell. You all won't even notice it's there. You will assume it has been there for decades and does not work. The guards will not bring it to your attention. In fact, they often bet on how long it will take the arrestees to figure out that the phone actually works. Eventually, one of you will decide to test it out; once that happens, the floodgates will open, as the phone will offer your only reprieve. Those on the outside will remind you that you are human and loved, because those on the inside certainly will not.

Eventually, we will start calling names. It will happen sporadically. There will be no rhyme or reason to how the names are called. Women who enter the cell after you will be called to see a judge before you. You'll eventually learn that you should have solidified paid counsel hours earlier because—as you would expect—our courts also bend to capitalism.

After about eighteen hours of waiting and processing, your name will be called. Guards will escort you through hallways and stairwells to the courtroom where the judge presides, but no guard will look at you or speak to you. They will continue on with their conversations as if you are not even there; because, when you fall into Department of Corrections custody, you become nothing.

You'll be placed in one final holding cell, where you may have an opportunity to speak with your attorney. Your waiting period, at this stage, should not endure for too long. Eventually, your name will be called for the second-to-last time. A guard will escort you from this final holding cell to a bench inside of the courtroom. You'll see cameras because someone believed that your case was newsworthy. Your attorney will ask that press be excluded, but the court will deny his application; and your name will be called one final time: *People of the State of New York v. Bianca Forde.* You'll get up; you'll walk towards your attorney, and given your lack of criminal history, I expect you'll get to go home.

But that will not be the end of it for you. These officers have made allegations that will affect your livelihood and your reputation in the legal community. Their allegations create the impression that you sought to use your position for a benefit. The prosecutor will take the officers' word for it and allow these allegations to be released to the public, despite the fact that you never uttered the words they claim you uttered. If you're lucky, someone will realize the difference between seeking special treatment, and vindicating your own Constitutional rights.

You will return to work; you will feel humiliated and judged; you will continue to remain on the payroll, but you will feel like a pariah; you will be denied the opportunity to speak in court, and – for a period of time – precluded from transitioning into a role that you earned. You will meet with high-ranking officials who will determine whether you are worthy of your title; you will consider leaving the department and leaving this world. You will lose yourself, but only for a moment.

One day, something will happen, and you will realize that this is not the end; it is the beginning. You will see how the bias of a bigot gifted you with a platform. Your misery will become your ministry: and your test, your testimony. You will embrace your obligation to share your perspective and experience in hopes of leaving the criminal justice system better than you found it. You will offer insight into how prosecutors, the most powerful actors in the criminal justice system, can, and must, use their power for good. It is true—your life will never be the same. It will be a life more rewarding than you could ever have imagined.

PART TWO: THE PARADOX

"In the most trying of times, remember you had a purpose before anyone had an opinion."

—UNKNOWN

CHAPTER 12: HOME SWEET HOME

Our first stop after my release was back to the precinct to reclaim my property. It was then that I realized how far the news had traveled. When I powered on my phone, I had texts and voicemails from friends who now resided all over the country. I could not wait to get to a computer to email the U.S. Attorney, and everyone else at the U.S. Attorney's Office that I felt needed to know. I knew many were likely already aware of my arrest given the press reports, but I needed them to know that I was not hiding from it; and further, that I was ready and willing to discuss the matter at their convenience.

We returned to my mother's home in Long Island around 8:00 p.m. or so. Some of my family members were already waiting for me. More would arrive shortly thereafter. I was now completely surrounded by love. I knew it was love because, for the last eighteen hours, I knew how it felt not to be. I shared about what I'd been through—laughing as I recounted tales about Isis, crying as I thought about the moment that my arms were pressed behind my back and my wrists bound. These were my people; the ones that would love and support me, unconditionally and relentlessly; the ones that would see through the bogus headlines.

As I sat there basking in their love, their positivity, and their adoration over my strength and resilience, I knew that I should savor every moment. I had several more crowds to address, and those individuals would be far less compassionate. Still, I could not wait to get out of New York and back to the District. I wanted badly to leave New York that night and head back to D.C., but my family convinced Joseph and me to get a good night's sleep. It's hard to disregard sound advice after spending a night in jail — especially given how much my family had already worried. So, we obliged. We decided to get some rest and leave early in the morning.

Around 4:00 a.m. the next morning (now Sunday), Joseph entered my childhood bedroom, and gently stirred me out of sleep. For an instant, everything was completely normal. I was normal. Life was normal. It took a few seconds to recall the prior twenty-four hours, and to realize that it had not been a dream. I had been arrested, spent the prior night in jail, and had become national news. I got dressed, uncertain about what my new reality would entail, but pleased to know that I did not have to face it quite yet. I had taken the week off months earlier, and decided not to cancel the vacation time, despite cancelling my trip.

I was supposed to fly to Dubai the night of my release, but I decided that boarding that flight was not in my best interest. The trip was to celebrate my good friend, Ann, who would soon be moving to London. I would also have the chance to reconnect with the friends I made while living and working in Dubai. We hadn't seen each other for a few years, but we always managed to pick up right where we left off. Still, I knew there was no way I could go to Dubai and enjoy myself. It was too soon, and my arrest still weighed on me too heavily. There were conversations that I needed to have within my office, conversations that I hoped would clear my name.

After returning to D.C., I clung to Joseph. We were in our own little cocoon—the safest place on earth. That Monday, we decided we would go see *Queen and Slim*, the movie — a 2020, "Black Lives Matter" rendition of Bonnie and Clyde. A fictional, yet realistic, illustration of how easily police encounters with Black citizens can go wrong. Minutes into the movie, Queen and Slim, played by Jodie Turner-Smith and Daniel Kaluuya, respectively, were pulled over for failing to use a turn signal and alleged erratic driving. To say Queen's character resonated with me would be an understatement.

Queen was a Black female and a criminal defense attorney. Her role as an attorney, in particular, practicing criminal law, was essential to her character in the film. There is a certain level of deference and leeway that lay people give officers. This deference is not given out of respect for the position, but out of fear. It allows officers to toe the line between what is and is not constitutional. It allows them to blur the lines between what is and is not voluntary; what is and is not consensual. When you're Black, you know your rights, and you're an attorney no less, you have a healthy degree of skepticism for the police. More importantly, you are not afraid to express it.

When the officer ordered Slim to "put [his] hand down, Queen interjected, noting his hands would not be up, but for the light the officer was shining in Slim's face. When the officer chastised Slim for narrating his movements, Queen explained it was necessary because, when it comes to Black people, police often "shoot now and ask questions later." Queen, without question, had a healthy skepticism for law enforcement, and she was unafraid to express it.

I remember the look of concern on Queen's face when Slim was asked to step out of the car. I recall her asking whether the officer had a warrant, as he rifled through the shoeboxes in the trunk of Slim's car. I remember how she stayed inside of the car, until she couldn't. "I am an attorney, and I demand to know why he is under arrest. What is your name? What is your badge number? I am reaching for my cell phone," she said. Seconds later, shots rang out. The officer shot Queen in the leg; Slim reacted in her defense, and the scene ends with the officer dead. If you do not know what happened next, I suggest that you rent the movie.

Some might call these facts extreme, but are they? As I watched Queen and Slim's police encounter play itself out, I replayed the events leading up to my arrest in my head. I relived the moment when Joseph was asked to step out of the car, and was guided to a position where I could not see or hear him. I re-experienced the anger and the fear. As tears fell from my eyes, I realized that we were fortunate to be alive.

I felt my work phone buzz at that precise moment. It was the chief of the USAO Criminal Division, requesting a phone meeting to go over "logistics." I suggested an in-person meeting. I was not certain of what these "logistics" referred to, but it definitely was not something that I planned to discuss over the phone. It was the beginning of several conversations that I would have with superiors within the department — all white men. Would they get it? Or would the world of *Queen & Slim* be too foreign to them. I guess time would tell.

CHAPTER 13: A "REPRESENTED PARTY"

On Wednesday, I met with our office's second-in-command, who I'll call the Deputy. He and I were not strangers. We had interacted on several occasions. The Deputy knew my name; he knew my reputation; he knew I was a respected AUSA. I was an active member of the office's Diversity Committee, which he chaired. I was a recent addition to the office's Hiring Committee. Further, I had been selected for a senior spot in our office's elite Fraud and Public Corruption Unit. I had proven myself, and I hoped that I had earned some grace.

Hours before meeting with the Deputy, I learned that a white male prosecutor had been arrested in D.C. on similar allegations a few weeks before my arrest, but our office had not papered the case. I was also aware of an incident involving a white male attorney accused of jury tampering in a homicide case, who the office appeared to protect at all costs. I was eager to see how I would be treated.

I thought long and hard about what I wanted to convey to the Deputy at our meeting. I was not certain that I would be asked for details but, to the extent I could fill-in any gaps missed by the media's account of the incident—and there were many—I would be happy to do so. I was intent on making the Deputy understand what, as a privileged white male, he instinctively might not. But he did not ask for details, and when I attempted to "offer context", he quickly interjected, reminding me that I was now "a represented party."

One of the first lessons you learn as a prosecutor is never to speak with a represented party. The rule is intended to protect the constitutional rights of the accused, in particular, the right against self-incrimination, and to maintain a standard of ethics amongst law enforcement. In my early days as a prosecutor, my adherence to the rule was a bit extreme. If an unfamiliar person approached me in the courthouse, my first question would be "do you have counsel?" If they replied "yes," I would immediately tell them that I could not speak with them. It did not matter how benign their query; e.g., "excuse me, do you know where the vending machine is?" I would respond, "I'm sorry, but you'll have to ask your attorney."

As obvious as it was that I sat in the Deputy's office that Wednesday morning as a defendant in a criminal case, the significance of that fact had not yet hit me before the words "represented party" came out of his mouth. In the eyes of the law and rules of ethics, my position had changed. I was not Bianca Forde, the prosecutor, the valued member of the USAO-DC team; I was now on the other side of the "v." Thus, before I could share the details of my arrest with any member of the USAO or DOJ, my attorney would have to provide written consent. The Deputy had done the ethical thing, the constitutional thing, for sure; but that fact did not make the status I now held in the eyes of my colleagues any easier to accept.

The conversation continued. "No one is taking any sides," he assured me, "but while this plays out, it is probably best for you to avoid court. *What do you think?*"

Mere days had passed since my arrest; it was my first time in the office since the incident. That morning, on my way to meet with the Deputy, I saw a handful of colleagues—many of whom would show empathy and support, and many who said nothing. It was impossible to tell whether their silence resulted from indifference, judgment, or simply not knowing what to say. I realized that just being in the office triggered my trauma, so I knew I was not ready to be in court.

"Yes, avoiding court makes sense to me," I responded to him. In retrospect, I should have suggested we put a time limit on that prohibition. Also, what was this about no one "taking sides"? *"Of course, you should be taking a side,"* I thought, *"my side!"*

The conversation continued. "You've clearly earned yourself a spot in the criminal division," referring to the federal-facing division of our office. "There is plenty for you to do there without going to court." Before our meeting, I feared I would be relegated to the intake unit of our Superior Court division until the N.Y.C. matter was resolved. I was relieved to know that option was not on the table.

"Cyber has work; VCNT (Violent Crime Narcotics Trafficking Unit) has work." I did not want to push my luck, but I had to ask, *"What does this mean for my move to Fraud & Public Corruption (FPC)?"* He made it clear that was a discussion for a later day. And so, for the next several months, I would bide my time on the Fourth Floor, in our office's Violent Crime Narcotics Trafficking Unit. I would not step foot in court, except to observe. I would watch other AUSAs handle cases that I had investigated and took to trial. "Bianca Forde for the United States"— a phrase I took delight in uttering —would go unheard and unspoken for the foreseeable future.

What initially afforded me an opportunity to get beyond the trauma of my arrest (e.g., time away from public view) eventually became demoralizing. I was essentially on desk duty; the aspects of my job that I loved most were no longer a part of my experience; and I was forced to spend my time investigating minor gun offenses that our office had chosen to charge federally for reasons that I resented wholeheartedly. Some might say I should have been grateful that I was allowed to keep my job while the criminal matter played itself out. My view of the world has never been that limited.

Amidst the uncertainties in my own professional life, our office was experiencing substantial internal turmoil. We lost our U.S. Attorney, who I valued and respected despite certain policy-based differences of opinion. In her place, we were given a presidential appointee, who appeared to share forty-five's shortcomings and temperament. It would soon come to light that he was solely hired to do the DOJ's dirty work, and another interim U.S. Attorney would replace him in a few short months. In addition, unprecedented DOJ interference in certain high-profile cases involving Trump allies would disappoint and humiliate prosecutors around the country; As much as I missed saying "Bianca Forde on behalf of the United States," the novelty and grandeur of being a federal prosecutor was no longer what it once was.

CHAPTER 14: THE ASSAULT ON MY NAME

I loved the sound of my name long before I was "Bianca Forde for the United States." Growing up, Grandma Lucille often talked about my grandfather, Walter. My grandfather was a respected prison officer in Guyana. Until writing this book, I had never stopped to think about the law enforcement connection I shared with my granddad. At some point, Grandpa Walter was the superintendent of several jails. I would have loved to speak with him about what jails in Guyana were like, and about the Guyanese philosophy on incarceration. Were incarceration and incapacitation the punishment, or were prison conditions as dire and deplorable as they are in the U.S.? Grandpa Walter died years before I was born; his death was likely the impetus for Grandma Lucille's migration to these United States.

Grandfather Walter was tall, he was handsome, and he was proud. I often imagine a man with quiet confidence. The type that did not have to make noise to let you know that he had entered any space; you simply knew he was there. He was the type of man who made an impression without ever opening his mouth. He was a man of few words but, when he spoke, people listened. Growing up, that was what the Forde name symbolized for me: respect.

Grandma Lucille often boasted on my mom—constantly

reminding me that my mother was a favorite of her primary school schoolmaster. My mother, she said, was the only other child the schoolmaster allowed his own daughter to befriend. I believe that was Grandma Lucille's way of encouraging me to be more like my mother: reserved, mild-mannered, and deferential of all in authority. Her desire to rewire me aside, the story implied a level of respectability that my mother garnered at a young age. That dignity, integrity, and respect became synonymous with being a Forde.

Growing up, my uncles—my mother's brothers—were well-respected businessmen in Caribbean circles. Many referred to them as the "Forde boys". They owned a nightclub and restaurant for years in Flatbush, Brooklyn, which was highly patronized by Caribbean-expatriates. It is only fitting that decades later, my cousins and I were often referred to as the "Forde girls"—regarded in our respective circles as smart, respectable, and driven. We never had lots of money; but what we lacked in wealth, we made up for in ambition, tenacity, and character.

For all of these reasons, I have always loved my name; but for a period of time following my arrest, all of that changed. I could not hear my name without visualizing what had been written about me. I could not meet a new person without wondering whether they'd "Googled" me and prejudged me. I struggled to be at work, where I felt that some of my colleagues had forgotten the meaning of the phrase "innocent until proven guilty." I felt responsible for this assault on my family name and, even more so, the pain, worry, and distress it had all caused my mother. In the months following my arrest, I became a sliver of myself. Crying was a daily phenomenon. The uncertainty of my future consumed me. It was a different kind of sadness. Far worse than any disappointment or heartbreak I'd ever experienced. Nothing made it better. No one made it better. It felt as though I had hit rock bottom. In retrospect, I was probably suffering from some degree of post-traumatic stress disorder (PTSD).

In the midst of it all, I spoke with my sister Allana. Allana introduced me to a podcast—specifically, Oprah's Super Soul Conversations. She sent me an episode called *Transform your Life*, with Bishop T.D. Jakes. In it, Jakes discussed the difference between living life from a place of pain, and living from a place of transformation. The former is best described as focusing on what has happened to us and what was *done to* us. In the latter, we focus on who we are and whose we are. Jakes reminded listeners that, when living from a place of pain and allowing the actions of others to affect our destiny, we give our power away.

As I listened to those words, I knew that if I did not check myself, and do so quickly, my arrest would not just end up stealing eighteen hours of my liberty; it would steal my future. I had fallen in spirit, but it was time to get back up. For the next few months, I meticulously managed what I let into my space, and thus, into my soul. If I was in the car, an episode of Oprah's Super Soul Conversations was on queue. Bishop Jakes had reminded me that persecution was a prerequisite for success. The Lady Gaga episode illustrated that pain can be used as a platform. My forever first lady, Michelle Obama, reminded me that when the universe hands us a platform, we bear the responsibility of using it, and doing so responsibly for the betterment and enrichment of others. These real-life, modern-day overcomers made me feel more empowered and connected to my purpose than I had ever imagined.

Slowly, the universe began to confirm that my purpose predated anyone else's opinion. I became convinced that I had something to share with the world, and moreover, that the world was waiting on me to execute. From that point on, I forged forward, knowing that God places desires on our heart, and blesses us with gifts, not so that we can hoard them for our ourselves; but so that we can bless others. I accepted that my arrest was a necessary pit stop along my path. What was once seen as a setback was proving to be a divine, providential setup. My trajectory had changed, and I knew, without a shadow of a doubt, that all things would work together for my good.

CHAPTER 15: DEFINE DISGRACE

A few months before my arrest, I'd been selected to join the Fraud and Public Corruption ("FPC") Unit of USAO-DC. It was an honor, and an affirmation of my hard work, persistence, and ability. Still, it was exciting for other reasons. I had spent the prior four years prosecuting individuals birthed amidst circumstances that offered little choice, and fewer role models. Success for them was an uphill battle from the start, should they elect to strive for it. Those who "made it", would be the exception and not the rule. I expected that FPC would be different. My defendants would no longer be overwhelmingly young Black men and women. They would be privileged individuals fueled by greed rather than desperation. My efforts would now be focused on holding the powerful accountable for their conduct, much of which would be in breach of public trust.

But all of that was now on hold. I could not try cases; I could not speak in court, and my move to FPC appeared to be perpetually on pause, pending resolution of the criminal case, and DOJ's investigation of the false report that called my ethics and character into question. I was a public corruption prosecutor accused of public corruption. The irony was not lost on me; nor was it lost on the DOJ.

By January, the Manhattan DA's Office decided my case was appropriate for an adjournment in contemplation of dismissal ("ACD") — a statutorily tool assumed to restore the accused to the position they were in prior to arrest. Pursuant to the ACD, the case is dismissed and sealed. A case resolved by ACD would usually remain open for six months, but Lance was able to negotiate a three-month waiting period. The criminal case would be over and untraceable by April 6, 2020, but for the internet.

Still, the ethical allegations concerned me the most. The complaint, quoting the officers' report, alleged that I had identified myself as a "U.S. Attorney,"—giving the impression that I had used my title and position for a benefit. The fact that I had never said those words was, apparently, of no consequence to the Manhattan DA's Office. In addition, I bore responsibility for explaining what was in my head when I presented my DOJ identification to the Rookie—specifically, why offering the one document in my possession that could prove I was a lawyer to an officer engaged in racial profiling, should not be construed as an effort to obtain a benefit. After all, rights and benefits were not the same. If demanding the right to be treated as any other motorist, irrespective of my race, could be construed as seeking a benefit, certainly I was living in a backwards universe and, moreover, working for the wrong agency.

In the coming weeks, I got the chance to explain these things to (you guessed it) a duo of white men. Only this time, they were both strangers to me. They knew nothing about me, other than what they had heard, read, or watched on body camera. I had the option of attending this meeting with Lance, but we both agreed that, optically, it was best for me to attend that meeting alone. There was a greater chance that, by attending alone, I would be seen as a fellow prosecutor and colleague, rather than as a mere target, subject, or "represented party."

On February 26, 2020, I woke up ready for what was possibly the most important meeting of my career. It was a meeting that would determine whether or not I had a future with the department; it would determine whether my departure from the U.S. Attorney's Office would be on my terms, or on those of someone else. I dressed for the occasion. I wore a tailored pink and black woolen blazer, with black fitted slacks and sleek black pumps. My hair was in a bun, my eyes lined, and my cheeks blushed and bronzed. They expected to meet the purported unruly Black woman; instead, they met AUSA Bianca M. Forde.

The lead attorney investigator, John, introduced himself to me in the lobby of 150 M. Street, N.E. During our meeting, he found a way to inject the fact that his wife is Puerto Rican — letting me know, in no uncertain terms that he got it; he could relate; he was *woke* (e.g., very aware). It quickly became evident that John and his co-investigator, an OIG agent, had made some assumptions about the case and about me. They incorrectly assumed that I must have planned to withhold the fact of my arrest from USAO personnel. In other words, why would I have been so upset by the search of my belongings but for the recovery of my DOJ credential? I guess the unconstitutional nature of the search was not enough to justify my outrage. They speculated that I must have said my title *at some point*, inaudibly, because it was not captured on the body camera—again deferring to the Arresting Officer rather than to their own ears and eyes. I got the sense they even expected me to lie about having shown my DOJ identification card to the Rookie—because they could not appreciate the difference between seeking a benefit, and demanding fair treatment.

At the end of the interview, John asked me whether I believe I had brought "disgrace on the department". The question caught me by surprise, to be honest. I wondered whether anyone had asked the officers involved in my case the same question. I wondered whether that question had been posed to the white male attorney in my office, who had attempted to orchestrate a guilty verdict by preying on the emotions of a mother awaiting the sentencing of her son. But John was asking about me. I leaned back in my chair, and I paused momentarily:

> No John, I do not. When I think back on that night, the way my partner and I were singled out as low-hanging fruit, and the fear I felt as I tried to figure out what was happening from inside of that car—no; I cannot conclude that I was the disgrace."

Had I successfully explained to the privileged white man with the Boricua spouse the realities of being Black in America, the realities of driving while Black, or the difference between a right and a benefit? Who knows? What I did know was that the longer I was forced to stay in the office's Violent Crimes and Narcotics Trafficking section—executing policies I wholeheartedly disagreed with—the less inclined I was to stick around to find out what John's investigation would conclude about AUSA Bianca M. Forde's fitness to serve.

CHAPTER 16: PERILOUS POLICY CHOICES

While I waited for the storm to pass, I remained in a holding pattern in the office's Violent Crimes and Narcotics Trafficking ("VCNT") section — a section that is sexy mostly in name only. In early 2019, the office tasked VCNT with prosecuting certain gun-possession cases under the U.S. Code's Felon-in-Possession ("FIP") statute, 18 U.S.C. Section 922(g). This federal provision makes it unlawful for any person previously convicted of a felony, to ship, receive, or possess a firearm in, through, or in a manner affecting interstate commerce. As there are no gun manufacturers physically located in the District of Columbia, there is a presumption that all guns recovered in D.C. have, at some point, moved through interstate commerce, e.g., crossed state lines. This presumption is the basis or "hook" that allowed USAO-DC to transfer the prosecution of these low-level, single-possession gun cases to federal court under a program titled "The FIP-Initiative."

Prior to 2019, Defendants arrested for the same conduct were charged in D.C. Superior Court under the D.C. Code's FIP statute. These cases were considered the most basic type of felony prosecution, and regarded as an introduction to jury trial practice for Tier 1 felony AUSAs. As there were no human victims, the stakes were much lower if things went awry, or so we were told.

The FIP defendants in Tier 1 were often represented by the D.C. Public Defender Service ("PDS"). While other public defender agencies around the country get a bad rap, and are assumed to be inept and under-qualified, D.C. PDS attorneys, for the most part, are the crème de la crème. They are talented and passionate lawyers who deeply believe in their work. Their primary downfall—and it is a major one—is playing fast and loose with the bar licenses of prosecutors. Other than that, I did not mind them. Defendants deserve zealous representation, and PDS is it.

Moving FIP cases from Superior Court to District Court, under the FIP-Initiative, was a policy shift with huge implications. First, it exposed similarly situated defendants to vast sentencing disparities, given that those sentenced under the United States Sentencing Guidelines often receive significantly longer sentences than their local counterparts. To be sure, public filings submitted by the ACLU and the D.C. Office of the Attorney General, relying on D.C. Council findings, declared that the average sentence imposed on locally charged Felon-in-Possession defendants between July 2017, and July 2018, was 20.89 months.[i] In stark contrast, the average sentence imposed on Felon-In-Possession defendants charged federally during the same period was 64 months.[ii]

The policy also disproportionately affected African Americans in the District. Rather than charging all defendants who met the FIP statutory criteria under the new policy, the office had, instead, cherry-picked amongst D.C. police districts—choosing to expose only those defendants arrested in the Blackest and poorest districts to the policy (e.g., police districts 5, 6, and 7). For obvious reasons, this cherry-picking was not widely publicized. Somehow, D.C.'s aggressive Public Defender's Service remained oblivious to how the policy was actually being enforced. Indeed, I was weeks into my VCNT detail before I was made aware of this selective law enforcement strategy.

While the office considered the FIP-Initiative to be an appropriate response to the District's rising and startling homicide rate,[iii] it is unclear what analysis or research the office undertook to assess whether the policy could be relied upon to solve the problem it purported to solve. Such research efforts may have indicated that the increase in homicides was due in large part to the lethality of guns in the District rather than to an increase in shootings.[iv] Such an analysis may have also revealed that an unusually high number of prior-year homicide investigations concluded in 2018, and were included in the 2018 calculations.[v] It is difficult to see how increasing the penalty for FIP defendants could be considered an effective law enforcement strategy under either scenario. The FIP-Initiative was obviously a knee-jerk policy reaction, unsupported by empirical data—no different from other "tough on crime" policies that have fueled the nation's mass-incarceration crisis and the prison industrial complex for decades.

I thought about the people who must have been sitting around the table at the time that the policy was proposed, and whether any had the courage to speak up against it. I wondered whether any had even recognized the inevitable disproportionate racial impact that the FIP-Initiative would have in poor, Black communities. To this day, the FIP-Initiative remains one of the clearest, most direct examples in my mind, of how the power of the prosecutor can be used to do harm rather than good.

One day, on my way home from work, I ran into another VCNT AUSA. She was preparing for a federal FIP trial, and griping about how much work these cases require. She commented on the countless hours that must be spent reviewing and disclosing body-worn camera. She made sure to tell me that she wasn't *complaining*, given that these FIP prosecutions provide a "great way to get your feet wet in federal court." They're an "easy" first district court trial; a good way to get to know the quirks and idiosyncrasies of the federal judges—it reminded me of how we described the cases in Tier 1.

As she went on and on about how the FIP-Initiative aided the transition of AUSAs from Superior Court to District Court, I wondered whether she had ever thought about the FIP-Initiative from the perspective of the accused, and so I inquired: "What are your thoughts on the fact that young Black boys are now facing three to four times more incarceration than they would in Superior Court because of the office's choice in venue?" She looked at me, bewildered. "That's a fair point," she said. "I guess I'd never thought about it that way." And with that, we parted ways.

Months later, I would have the opportunity to ask a senior member of criminal division leadership what, if any, investigative steps the office was taking—in coordination with our law enforcement partners—to investigate and disrupt the flow of firearms into D.C. After all, no one disputed that the guns were entering the district primarily through Maryland and Virginia. He responded, "those guns are coming in through straw-men" (e.g., those who fraudulently and illegally acquire guns on behalf of others to conceal the true buyer's identity)—as if that fact made those cases and individuals unworthy of investigation.

I understood him to mean that pursuing such cases would be too difficult and time consuming. Identifying straw-purchasers would indeed require multi-agency coordination, surveillance, and significant law enforcement resources. The prosecution of the young, Black man on the wrong side of South Capitol Street with a pistol in his pants, however, required none of these things. This category of defendant—who consents to the pat-down because he knows the mere act of turning away, or "appearing nervous," will be used to justify a search—is the low hanging fruit; and against him—and primarily him—the full force of our law enforcement prowess would be deployed.

CHAPTER 17: THE RECKONING

Every *Gerstein* affidavit, for every gun possession case ever, started about the same. For example:

On February 15, 2020, members of the Metropolitan Police Department (MPD) Gun Recovery Unit (GRU) were on patrol in the 1300 block of Alabama Avenue, S.E., PSA 705, a known high-crime area, wearing plain clothes marked with "POLICE" identifiers, and operating an unmarked vehicle. There, they observed a White Lexus Sedan, Tag No. 123ABC, driving westbound on Alabama Avenue, S.E., toward 14th Street, S.E.

After stating the setting, the affidavit explained why the individual, soon to be identified as the "defendant," caught GRU's attention; i.e., the facts supporting "reasonable suspicion." They often read something like this: "Officer X immediately noticed that the front passenger windows and windshield appeared to be above the legal tint limit for vehicles operating in the District of Columbia and, based on that observation, he activated his emergency lights to initiate a traffic stop." If I had a dollar for every time a traffic stop was premised on an illegal tint, I could retire.

Eventually, the GRU officers all exit their unmarked car, and approach different sides of the civilian vehicle. The Officers will speak with each occupant until any little thing gives them a reason to convert a ticket-able offense into an arrestable one. The *Gerstein* affidavit would state:

> While speaking with the front seat passenger, identified by his Washington, D.C. identification card as Christopher Smith, Officer Y observed that Smith appeared nervous. Concerned for his safety, and that of the other officers, Officer Y asked Smith to step out of the car. Officer X asked the driver, identified by his Washington, D.C. driver's license as Patrick Jones, to do the same.

At this point, it was only a matter of time until an officer conducted a pat down for "officer safety" and felt something that he believed "in his training and experience to be contraband;" or called for a K9 unit based on an inchoate "hunch" that *something illegal* was in the car. Alternatively, the officer might ask the occupants, unaware of their rights, to consent to a search. More times than not, occupants give consent, either because they do not realize they can say "no," or because they believe that saying "no" will have no impact. In other words, the police will do whatever they want anyway and rationalize it after the fact.

In an article titled "Thin Blue Lies: How Pretextual Stops Undermine Police Legitimacy," Jonathan Blanks discusses how these pretextual stops contribute to mistrust of law enforcement, especially in African American communities.[i] Blanks writes:

> Many of those invasive and unpleasant stops are legal under existing case law, thereby leaving the subjects of those stops with no recourse in court. Many Black people who are stopped understand or believe that the potential

cost of saying no to an officer could result in officer agitation—resulting . . . in handcuffs or worse—and a belief the officer may end up searching the car anyway. Under these circumstances, while consent is "voluntarily given" in the eyes of the law, it does not feel that way to those people giving it. [ii]

Reviewing the *Gerstein* affidavits (e.g., probable cause statements) for FIP cases made me painfully aware that—if we are not careful—we can enter prosecution with an eye toward public service and justice, but end up as mere pawns perpetuating centuries of systemic racial injustice. In the words of John, my OIG Investigator, the FIP-Initiative most certainly brought disgrace upon the department; but more shame-inducing moments were around the corner.

In February 2020, something unprecedented happened in the case of *U.S. v. Roger Stone*. Stone, the white, rich, politically connected Trump ally, had been charged and convicted of lying to Congress, witness tampering, and obstructing an official proceeding. The prosecutors who handled the case, were closest to the facts, and sat through every moment of the trial, recommended a guidelines-compliant sentence of seven to nine years. Soon thereafter, they were publicly vetoed by the DOJ on the grounds that a guidelines-compliant sentence was "extreme and excessive and disproportionate" in Stone's particular case.

It was an infuriating time for any federal prosecutor who ever held her position in high esteem. How could any prosecutor credibly claim to have power, or discretion, when it was possible for DOJ personnel to override the line prosecutor on a whim, solely based on the political clout of the person charged? By interjecting themselves on behalf of Roger Stone, the Justice Department signaled that the guidelines were too punitive for a white, rich, upper-class man, but completely appropriate for the poor, Black man selectively prosecuted in police district 7. I was angry, frustrated, and ashamed.

Just one week prior to the Stone saga, I moderated a panel called "Changing the Narrative: Strategies and Tactics to End Racially Disproportionate and Mass Incarceration," on behalf of the National Black Prosecutors' Association. There was one former D.C. Public Defender Service (PDS) attorney on the panel who had transitioned into a role with the Justice Collaborative, a public interest organization focused on criminal justice reform. When asked how prosecutors can use their power and discretion to rebalance the scales of justice, this former PDS attorney responded:

> I don't think the way to fight mass incarceration is to be a line prosecutor . . . that is because of the systemic challenges that are already in place. . . I think that it is exceptionally hard in most prosecutors' offices currently to . . . by just doing your job be advancing the system.

I have to admit that I cringed as I heard those words. Certainly, the way to improve the system was not to steer fair, justice-minded lawyers away from the field of prosecution. My social awareness had most certainly benefited the lives of the defendants added to my docket. But maybe there was some truth to those remarks; maybe I was fighting the right fight, but on the wrong battlefield; maybe it was time to face the fact that the highlight of my career might not be trying a corrupt politician who used his power, or the public's purse, for self-gain; or a civil rights case with the Chief of Fraud and Public Corruption, who I adored. I started to consider that maybe the universe had something else in store for me; maybe it was inviting me to reframe the narrative around prosecution as we know it, in an effort to create a justice system that we could actually be proud of for generations to come—a system where the young, Black man on the wrong side of South Capitol street, and a presidential ally, are truly deemed equal under the law.

PART THREE: THE PLAN

"But recall those earlier days when, after you had been enlightened, you endured a hard struggle with sufferings, sometimes being publicly exposed to abuse and persecution, and sometimes being partners with those so treated. Do not, therefore, abandon that confidence of yours; it brings a great reward."

—HEBREWS 10:32–34 & 35

A PREFACE TO THE PLAN

S o, you want to be a prosecutor. You apply to a local or federal prosecutor's office. You go through the interview process—one like no other, designed to assess how you think, what kind of prosecutor you will be, and whether your tendency is to default to honesty or deception.

It is a process mired with hypotheticals, created to determine whether you can be trusted with the vast discretion that will be bestowed upon you, should you be selected to serve. If I am your interviewer, my primary objective is to deduce whether you are likely to leave the system better than you found it, or simply use it as a means of advancing your own ambition, as is often the case.

It is common to hear former federal prosecutors boast that the years they spent as Assistant U.S. Attorneys (AUSAs) were the most professionally rewarding years of their careers. Yet, so many return to private practice after just a few years of service. Most of the prosecutors I knew, before becoming one, were law firm partners. Many had started their careers at law firms. As mid-level or senior associates, they had taken a detour through a U.S. Attorney's office, a detour through which they hoped to gain coveted trial and investigation experience. They believed such experience and exposure would distinguish them from their peers, against whom they would ultimately compete for partnership.

During my last week as a law firm associate, a female partner and former AUSA cautioned me to make every moment count professionally while in government. "Get the right experience, and get it fast," she admonished. This approach would make up for the massive pay cut I would be taking, which she assumed would be temporary. Surely my goal was to return to the firm, right?

This advice, while well intentioned, encourages law firm associates to view the role of prosecutor as a prelude or prerequisite to a lucrative, white-collar career in private practice. This self-serving desire to obtain trial stats, and the skillset necessary to secure a book of business, is entirely at odds with the role of the prosecutor, which is to serve. Entering the field of prosecution with a mindset of transience makes it impossible to take any real interest or ownership in the system—the type of interest and ownership conducive to advancing justice, rather than maintaining the status quo. Thus, when prosecutors' offices set their sights on law firm associates—who often have the highest test scores and law school grade point averages—they forget that those quantitative measurements do not necessarily translate into good judgment, or even common sense—essential traits of a fair, balanced, *Berger* prosecutor.

In 1935, the U.S. Supreme Court explained the role of the prosecutor in the seminal case, *United States v. Berger*:

> The [prosecutor] is the representative not of an ordinary party to a controversy, but of a sovereignty whose obligation to govern impartially is as compelling as its obligation to govern at all; and whose interest, therefore, in a criminal prosecution is not that it shall win a case, but that justice shall be done. As such, he is in a peculiar and

very definite sense the servant of the law, the twofold aim of which is that guilt shall not escape or innocence suffer. He may prosecute with earnestness and vigor-indeed, he should do so. But, while he may strike hard blows, he is not at liberty to strike foul ones. It is as much his duty to refrain from improper methods calculated to produce a wrongful conviction as it is to use every legitimate means to bring about a just one.[i]

While *Berger* expressly addressed the role of the federal prosecutor, it's wisdom can and should be extended to all levels of prosecution. In a perfect world, prosecutors would spend months understanding how to exercise their discretion in a way that aligns with Judge Sutherland's vision for the role of prosecutor. But this is not a perfect world. Prosecutors' offices around the country are overworked and understaffed. New prosecutors are trained by already-stretched chief prosecutors who lack the time to teach beyond the bare minimum of what the rules require—the absolute "do's and don'ts" one must know to avoid being sanctioned by a judge, or cited by the bar. They do not have time to teach the gray. Similarly, overworked prosecutors do not have time to think critically; rather, they do what they are told, or what has been done before. They learn on the job—at the expense of the person accused—and there are few combinations more threatening than lack of knowledge coupled with power.

Much has been written about the power of the American prosecutor. In a 2005 article, Dr. Angela J. Davis refers to prosecutors as "the most powerful officials in the American criminal justice system. The decisions they make control the operation of the system, and often predetermine the outcome of criminal cases."[ii] Similarly, in one of the most influential books of the last decade, *The New Jim Crow: Mass Incarceration in the Age of Colorblindness,* Michelle Alexander describes the prosecutor as "the most powerful law enforcement official in the criminal justice system."[iii] It's not the judge, and not the police, Alexander writes. "It is the prosecutor, far more than any other criminal justice official, who holds the keys to the jail-house door."[iv]

To put this into perspective, the fact that a police officer makes an arrest does not obligate the prosecutor to take any action. The prosecutor may decline to file charges or choose to file alternative charges. The prosecutor may even institute a grand jury investigation, which allows her to investigate the matter in secret, without alerting the target or the community that an investigation is underway. Once a criminal case becomes public, the prosecutor's decisions determine the degree to which the liberty interest of the accused is restrained, and the length of any liberty restriction imposed.

At all stages—from arrest through trial, plea and sentencing—the prosecutor bears responsibility for all aspects of the legal case. She elects whether to offer a plea, when the plea should be extended, and what the plea offer should be. While the defense may submit a counteroffer, the prosecutor is under no obligation to accept it—leaving the accused with one of two choices: take her offer or go to trial.

While myriad rules govern the prosecutor's disclosure obligations, she enjoys considerable flexibility in determining when those disclosures are made. She may impose restrictions on how disclosed material is used by the defense. While the judge ultimately imposes the sentence, the prosecutor's charging decision may preordain the defendant's exposure, for instance, by charging offenses that carry mandatory minimum sentences, and thus tying the judge's hands.

Finally, at any stage of a proceeding, the prosecutor can, without explanation, seek the dismissal of a case. And when asked why, after all of these months, she has elected not to go forward, she can simply say: "Prosecutorial discretion, Your Honor." It goes without saying that the power of the prosecutor is vast, and it is virtually unchecked by anyone, other than senior and supervisory prosecutors.

The realities of these powers, and the impact that they have had and continue to have on how "justice" happens in the U.S., cannot be overstated. Accordingly, prosecutors play a crucial role in dismantling the system of racially disproportionate and mass incarceration. We (prosecutors nor society) can no longer condone the learn-on-the-job approach that characterizes most prosecutors' offices, or the failure of prosecutors' training programs to meaningfully educate new recruits on race, class, socioeconomic privilege, implicit bias, stereotype bias, status-quo bias, and other matters intrinsic to understanding the needs and circumstances of the communities that they serve. If we are to overcome the new caste system that Alexander describes,[v] prosecutors are in the best position to do so, but only if they are trained early and often on how to use their unfettered power for good.

We are Uniquely Primed for Change in this Moment

Many historians have theorized that societies are best primed for social and cultural change following the destruction and devastation caused by war.[vi] And while the destruction and devastation brought about by COVID-19, coupled with the myriad instances of police brutality against unarmed Black men and women in 2020, do not qualify as "war" in the traditional sense, these realities have made it impossible to deny the vast, far-reaching racial and socioeconomic inequalities that plague our institutions—including the justice system. Moreover, the handling of the deaths of Ahmaud Arbery, Breonna Taylor, George Floyd, and others have confirmed and—in some cases—

introduced the community at large to the power of prosecutorial discretion.

On February 23, 2020, Ahmaud Arbery, age twenty-six, was gunned down during his daily afternoon jog by two white men, father and son. The father, a former detective, had a relationship with the prosecutor's office that initially declined to charge the duo—concluding that they had stood their ground under Georgia law. This decision was made despite video evidence showing Arbery being chased and hunted like prey by these two predators. A prosecutor made that initial decision.

On March 13, 2020, officers of the Louisville Metro Police Department in Kentucky executed a "no knock" warrant at the home of Breonna Taylor and Kenneth Walker. The two were asleep when they heard officers enter. Believing their home was being burgled, Mr. Walker fired his licensed firearm. Police then unleashed a volley of bullets, striking Taylor multiple times and killing her. Walker was originally charged with attempted murder on grounds that a 9mm bullet expelled from his firearm struck an officer in the thigh; it was alleged that *only* Walker possessed a 9mm firearm that night. We would later learn that one of the involved-officers was also carrying a 9mm handgun. While charges have been filed for placing Taylor's neighbors at risk, no police officer has been charged in Taylor's death. I attribute this injustice to how prosecutors chose to move forward with that case.

On May 25, 2020, a Minneapolis Police Department (MPD) officer knelt mercilessly on the neck of George Floyd while fellow MPD officers either watched or assisted. Mr. Floyd's loved ones, the nation, and the world have now seen the final moments of Mr. Floyd's life, as he lay prostrate on the pavement, gasping for air and pleading for his life. It took days to make an arrest, even in the presence of damning video evidence. All officers involved have now been charged because of a series of decisions made by prosecutors.

I describe these incidents not to incense or enrage—although they should do both. I describe them to impress upon you the vast power of the prosecutor, and how essential it is that the individuals ordained with this power are selected wisely and trained to see the *gray*. As the most powerful actors in the criminal justice system, prosecutors bear the onus of transforming a system that often does more harm than good. While some reformists believe that the phrase "justice-minded prosecutor" is an oxymoron, that perspective is, at best, inaccurate, and at worst, dangerous. It is dangerous in that it deters generations of justice-minded lawyers and law students away from the field of prosecution.

Given that the institution of the prosecutor shows no signs of being overthrown anytime soon, we must recruit, and train prosecutors to behave as justice-minded servants of the law. We must empower them to do what is fair, right, and humane. We must instill in them the principles of *Berger*, early and often, so that they understand the magnitude of their role and the needs of communities they serve. The lessons that follow are designed to do just that.

These lessons do not compromise the prosecutor's public safety mandate, nor do they put victims last. To the contrary, these lessons stem from a recognition that the prosecutor's role as servant of the law entails obligations to the victim, and also to the accused; obligations that are neither in-conflict, nor mutually exclusive. We can continue to protect the community and vindicate victims, without fueling deeply ingrained racial and socioeconomic imbalances in the criminal justice system. We can and we must. These lessons reveal how.

LESSON 1: UNPACK THE "SERVANT OF THE LAW" MANDATE

Privilege exists in many forms. A two-parent home is a privilege; a life without exposure to drug use or physical abuse is a privilege; having role models and mentors who counteract negative and antisocial influences or, alternatively, being shielded from such influences entirely, are privileges.

As a prosecutor, you will encounter individuals from all walks of life, whose life experiences will look nothing like your own. Whether you can relate to them or not, your job is to empathize, and when you have the power to improve someone's life condition for the better, you must do so. While you will find no procedural or ethical rule to that effect, that is your mandate as a servant of the law.

One of my most misguided moments as a prosecutor occurred within months of becoming one. At the time, I was assigned to the Misdemeanor Domestic Violence trial section of the U.S. Attorney's Office for the District of Columbia (USAO-DC). I had been asked to handle a case involving second-degree child abuse of an eight-year-old girl by the child's mother. The matter came to our attention after a schoolteacher observed bruises on the child, some fresh and some old. During our investigation, we spoke with a sibling of the victim who reported that many of the bruises were caused when their mother, in a rage, struck the victim repeatedly with a broom. The beating continued, even as the child sought coverage under a bed. I was instantly outraged.

The defendant's attorney was a court-appointed Black woman we will call Hailey. Hailey pleaded with me for diversion, so that her client would not have to enter into a guilty plea or risk a conviction at trial. Diversion is similar to probation, but it occurs in lieu of a plea or trial. Under a diversion agreement, a defendant must complete certain conditions, such as anger management, drug and alcohol treatment, or parenting classes, to name a few. Upon completion of the required conditions, the case is dismissed and the arrest is sealed. If she violates her conditions for instance, by missing a court date, or getting re-arrested, the government can rescind the agreement and reinstitute the criminal charge.

Hailey claimed that, at the time of the incident, the mom had been under tremendous pressure, but she was now ready to turn her life around. Hailey appealed to my sense of compassion, explaining that, if convicted, the mom could lose her home and even her children. I recall thinking, *well, maybe she should*. My mind was made up. That mother had crossed the line and she would either enter into a plea, or go to trial. However, before the case could be resolved, I rotated to a different trial unit, and another AUSA was put in charge of the defendant-mom's case. That AUSA, a white man, offered diversion.

I later learned that the AUSA who inherited the case had a personal and complicated relationship with abuse that likely framed the way he viewed defendant-mom. His personal experience had taught him a version of the *gray* that I did not know. His life experience allowed him to empathize in a way that I could not at that time and, as a result of that empathy, defendant-mom was given a second chance. But criminal justice outcomes cannot hinge on whether the prosecutor's life experience mirrors that of the accused because, in most cases, the two will not align. Rather prosecutors' offices must appropriately train line prosecutors to understand the needs and circumstances of the communities they serve. Such training is the only way the exercise of empathy will become systemic.

I do not know what became of that family. I do not know whether that young, struggling mother completed the conditions of diversion successfully, and became a better caregiver as a result. I would like to think that all of those things are true, for the sake of that then-eight-year-old girl and the other children in the household. What I do know, is that I had taken an uncompromising approach and, in doing so, I missed an opportunity to assess what justice ought to look like in that particular case. I missed an opportunity to use my discretion to improve the circumstances of an entire family. At no point did I consider what, if any, resources I had at my disposal to do so; at no point was I taught to take any of that into consideration. While no rule required me to ask that of myself, it is an example of the *gray*; *gray* that I was too inexperienced to recognize, *gray* overshadowed by my personal outrage at the conduct of the woman accused.

Months later, I was sworn in as an AUSA. During the ceremony, a prominent public official cautioned us as follows:

> While you have many cases, your victims likely only have one. That one case—albeit one of many for you—is their one and only. It keeps them up at night. It has potential to affect their physical security, and their finances. So be patient with your victims; lead with kindness, even when you are at your wits' end; return their phone calls; choose empathy over judgment. That is my charge to you today.

This advice is not only relevant to the prosecutor's conduct vis-à-vis victims. I believe this advice must be instilled in prosecutors with respect to the accused. The variety of factors that lead one to become entangled in the criminal justice system are nuanced and complex, and often far beyond the ken of the privileged prosecutor—hence why the terms *victim* and *defendant* are fluid.

Most individuals charged in street-level crime began life from a position of disadvantage. Pre-sentence reports, provided to the parties and the court weeks before a defendant is sentenced, confirm this. These reports detail the upbringing, education, finances, and overall history of the accused. As a felony AUSA handling violent crimes, I learned, per these reports, that many of the defendants I prosecuted were reared by drug addicts, or had no parents at all. They experimented with drugs at an early age, and developed addictions they carried into adulthood. Many witnessed abuse, or suffered it. They grew up in circumstances plagued by poverty that predisposed them to criminal contacts. They lived in over-policed communities, which led to unfairly inflated arrest records and convictions for conduct that goes unpunished in rich, suburban communities. The crimes they committed were either crimes of desperation, or crimes modeled for them. And, once they entered the system, their life situation only became worse.

For instance, post-conviction, an individual:

> [M]ay be ineligible for many federally funded health and welfare benefits, food stamps, public housing, and federal educational assistance. His driver's license may be automatically suspended, and he may no longer qualify for certain employment and professional licenses. If he is convicted of another crime, he may be subject to imprisonment as a repeat offender. He will not be

permitted to enlist in the military, or possess a firearm, or obtain a federal security clearance. If a citizen, he may lose the right to vote; if not, he becomes immediately deportable.[i]

Those who become entangled in the criminal justice system often have the least to lose. Our system responds by taking what little they have away, essentially giving them little choice but to recidivate. While it is easy to write off the accused as a product of their own free will and independent choice, the reality is that many of us did not make good choices; we had good options. There is a difference. The multitude of bad options presented to those who live in the communities we tend to target and over-police on a daily basis are unquantifiable. And so, when as prosecutors we have resources at our disposal to improve someone's life condition, whether they are a victim, a witness, or the accused, our mandate is to do so.

When prosecutors are trained to recognize and acknowledge these realities, they exercise their discretion differently. They are more inclined to make the case for diversion when justice so requires. They are less likely to pile on conditions of supervision that result in excessive, debilitating fees and requirements that set the accused up for failure. Training prosecutors to acknowledge these realities, and to align their exercise of discretion with the needs and circumstances of the communities they serve, is the first step toward dismantling racial and socioeconomic inequity in criminal justice.

LESSON 2: HOLD ROGUE OFFICERS ACCOUNTABLE

Identifying a predilection for or against police officers is so important that most criminal trials present three opportunities in which to do so. The first arises during the initial *voir dire* process, when every member of the jury pool is asked whether they can objectively and neutrally assess law enforcement testimony. The second occurs after the jury is sworn, before opening statements begin. At that time, the judge instructs jurors that law enforcement testimony should *not* be given more or less weight than any other type of witness testimony. The third arises at the close of trial, prior to deliberations, when the judge essentially reiterates the same instruction.

The purpose of these instructions is to ensure that law enforcement officer testimony is evaluated by the same standards that govern lay witness testimony. As with any lay witness, the jury may consider whether the officer or agent presents as a truthful person, with an accurate memory, or has any interest in the outcome of the case. The jury may also consider whether the officer or agent has been corroborated or contradicted by credible evidence. While our system emphasizes instilling these values in jurors, we must acknowledge that prosecutors are also susceptible to law enforcement bias, particularly when the matter involves an agent that the prosecutor respects, works with often, and considers a friend.

The "prosecution team" is now understood to include the law enforcement officers and agents involved in any investigation. That is because, in an ideal world, the prosecutors and agents assigned to any investigation work, in tandem, from the commencement of an investigation through the trial or plea, and sentencing. Case leads can occur without notice, so the lines of communication between prosecutor and agent are often open around the clock. It is not uncommon for the prosecutor–agent relationship to involve long hours, late nights, early mornings, weekend crime scene visits, and travel. This degree of contact breeds trust, solidarity, and friendship—all of which make the work more enjoyable, but also have a tendency to cloud judgment when bad acts occur.

Take Dawan Walker's case, for example. Walker was a twenty-something-year-old Black man charged with possession of an illegal firearm in D.C. Superior Court. Walker's case would be my first felony trial, and I was thrilled. After months of trying misdemeanor bench trials, I would get to present a case to a jury. My career as a trial lawyer was imminent.

A few days before the trial was scheduled to begin, I met with the lead officer, we'll call him Officer Fleetio. I had heard of Fleetio, but it was my first time meeting and working with him. He was reputed to be aggressive, and sort of a flirt. My first impression was that he presented as a privileged frat boy. At the time, he was assigned to MPD's Narcotics and Special Investigations Unit (NSID) and it was rumored that he was on the fast track to becoming a detective because his father held a respectable position within the department.

At our meeting, one of the first items on our agenda was preparing for a suppression hearing. The defense had moved to suppress the gun recovered from Walker on Fourth Amendment grounds, and I needed Fleetio to help me understand all of the facts relevant to the Fourth Amendment analysis. For instance, what drew his attention to Walker in the first place, when did he notice that Walker might be armed, and how did he go about confirming that? The facts stated in the *Gerstein* affidavit in support of probable cause would no longer be sufficient. I needed the play-by-play. It was game time.

Fleetio explained that he initially observed Walker in a crosswalk. He described Walker's clothing, e.g., blue jeans and a white T-shirt, and claimed Walker had displayed the "characteristics of an armed gunman"—a common law enforcement phrase. I asked him to elaborate. Fleetio began with a description of Walker's gait, explaining it in words I would hear time and time again, every time I was assigned to handle a case involving the recovery of a firearm.

> When most people walk, their hands swing from side to side. Often, those carrying guns use one hand to hold the weapon in place, as it is common for those carrying unregistered firearms not to use holsters. Bulky holsters increase opportunities for detection by the police.

Thus, according to Fleetio, when he observed Walker swinging one hand, while the other held his pants, Walker caught his eye.

Fleetio continued, "He was walking with a dramatic limp, which also suggest[ed] the presence of a large object causing interference with one's natural stride." I asked Fleetio to stand up and demonstrate. He obliged, and here is where it got interesting. His demonstration of Walker's gait was a sight to be seen. He limped across my office, raising his feet several inches above the floor with each step, his feet landing no less than thirty-six inches apart—leading anyone with common sense to wonder why someone carrying an illegal firearm would behave in a manner that would, undoubtedly, draw the attention of law enforcement. But I left it alone for the time being. After all, I was a rookie and it was my first felony trial. We finished up our prep session, and Fleetio left my office.

The evening before trial, I received video from a local convenience store that captured the crosswalk where Fleetio encountered Walker. Upon reviewing the video, I observed Walker. He was in a crosswalk, dressed just as Fleetio described, but there was nothing unusual about his gait. There was absolutely nothing that warranted Fleetio's suspicion that Walker was carrying a weapon.

I was somewhat oblivious to this reality then; but I now know that this is how police officers all over the country are trained to do their jobs. They see young Black men and women in poor communities as low-hanging fruit. They wouldn't dare drive through suburbs such as Georgetown demanding that suburban white boys lift their shirts to reveal their waistbands; yet they routinely engage in this targeted, harassing conduct in poor, Black neighborhoods. The worst part is that residents of these communities have come to accept this harassment as a way of life.

Under normal circumstances, this conduct goes uncorrected. After all, the Supreme Court has made it clear that police can approach any citizen, for any reason, to conduct what is often referred to as a "*Terry* stop." What made Walker's case different was that Fleetio embellished and I could prove it, even though the case pre-dated D.C.'s deployment of body-worn camera technology. It makes you wonder how often the rights of poor, Black men and women are trampled upon, without vindication, because there is no body-worn camera or private video footage available.

I really was not sure what to do. It was my first week handling felony cases. The trial was expected to begin the next day, and Fleetio was a far more experienced officer than I was a prosecutor. Perhaps I was missing something, but my gut told me something was off, so I asked a supervisor. Within an hour, three supervisors were in my office—all tuned into the surveillance video. One exclaimed, "Look, I see a limp." I responded, "Every guy in the hood walks like that." That "limp" was a far cry from what Fleetio had described.

Eventually, I received permission to dismiss the case. Not because my supervisors were deeply concerned with Walker's Fourth Amendment rights, or the ninety days he had already spent in custody. Their concern was that Fleetio's gross exaggeration would have to be disclosed to the defense, who would use that evidence to tank the case at trial. If the defense's cross-examination was effective, the judge would likely make a credibility finding against Fleetio, who might then be prohibited from testifying at future trials or from taking a meaningful role in any investigation going forward. Alternatively, if we dismissed the case and released Walker, no disclosures about Fleetio's transgressions would need to be made.

The following day, when asked by the judge why the prosecution had dismissed the case at this late stage, I responded as I'd been told to do: "Prosecutorial discretion, Your Honor." One week into being a felony prosecutor, it was lost upon me that the decision to dismiss the case was not to avenge the constitutional rights of Walker, but rather to protect Fleetio, and avoid giving the defense bar any ammunition to fuel the narrative of law enforcement distrust.

Within the next several months or so, Fleetio was found guilty in an administrative proceeding for conducting body cavity searches that violated both MPD protocol and the Fourth Amendment. He was ultimately dismissed from the department. Walker, on the other hand, would be arrested for the murder of an unarmed fourteen-year-old during a dice game. After Walker's re-arrest, two of my colleagues—a peer and a supervisor—suggested that the 14-year old's death was somehow on me for seeking dismissal of the Walker case. Neither acknowledged for one moment that Fleetio's corrupt conduct was to blame. It was Fleetio's interest in getting guns off of the street at any cost that put Walker in a position to possess and use a firearm.

This example makes clear that rogue and dishonest officers undermine legitimate law enforcement efforts, and place the community at risk in more ways than one. The prosecutor's job is not to protect rogue officers. We do the community a disservice when we are more concerned with preserving relationships with law enforcement partners than with justice. Our job is to prosecute without fear, favor, or prejudice; thus when we see misconduct, we must call it out, even when the perpetrator wears a uniform.

Further, the decision to dismiss or decline a case that arises from unconstitutional police misconduct is necessary, but not sufficient. While such decisions may limit the harm caused by the constitutional misstep, they do not sufficiently deter similar police misconduct in the future. Prosecutors are the best equipped to identify officers who play fast and loose with constitutional rights, and ensure appropriate consequences for such behavior. To be sure, Fleetio should have been trained in the first instance and monitored following the Walker case. Had he received such appropriate training, the community may have been spared further harassment, and Fleetio may still have a job. Instead, he continued to conduct his law enforcement duties as though he were above reproach, without fear of consequence for his distasteful behavior.

Prosecutors must be trained to identify officers like Fleetio. Similarly, prosecutors' offices must leverage data to track the frequency and degree of such violations, and the officers that commit them. Prosecutors are the first line of defense when the constitutional rights of the accused are violated; and, in many ways, are the gatekeepers of the justice system. When it comes to constitutional rights, the ends simply do not justify the means.

LESSON 3: LIBERTY IS A HUMAN RIGHT

I f our nation's founding documents are any indication, the only thing more important than liberty is life itself. This core American value is often reflected in the decisions of the U.S. Supreme Court.

In 1974, the Supreme Court decided *Gerstein v. Pugh*.[i] There, petitioners challenged the ability of prosecutors to deny bail and detain arrestees for extended periods of time, simply by filing charging documents. The court deemed the practice irreconcilable with the Fourth Amendment's requirement that probable cause be determined by a neutral magistrate. The Court recognized that allowing prosecutors to attempt to fill that role would entrust "the instruments of law . . . to a single functionary."[ii]

Further, the Court recognized that the involvement of the neutral magistrate must be prompt, noting the potentially devastating effects of pretrial detention. Indeed, "[p]retrial confinement may imperil the suspect's job, interrupt his source of income, and impair his family relationships." The court added that "[t]he consequences of prolonged detention may be more serious than the interference occasioned by arrest," and noted further that "[e]ven pretrial release may be accompanied by burdensome conditions that effect a significant restraint of liberty."[iii] Still, *Gerstein* did not define what constituted a timely and prompt determination of probable cause. The court did not answer that question for nearly two decades, with its 1991 decision in *County of Riverside v. McLaughlin*[iv].

In *Riverside,* a class of California arrestees challenged a statute that often resulted in delays as great as seven days before a neutral magistrate ruled on probable cause. There, the Court defined "timely and prompt" as forty-eight hours, concluding:

> We believe that a jurisdiction that provides judicial determinations of probable cause within forty-eight hours of arrest will, as a general matter, comply with the promptness requirement of *Gerstein.*

After *Riverside,* it was generally accepted that, once the arrestee was presented to a neutral magistrate within forty-eight hours, the charging entity was "immune" from challenge. However, no empirical data was provided for why forty-eight hours was considered reasonable. After all, what are the administrative steps inherent to an arrest that must be completed before an arrestee can be seen by a neutral magistrate? The Court did not answer that question. Even Justice Scalia viewed forty-eight hours as too flexible, urging that a twenty-four-hour period was, perhaps, the more appropriate boundary for issuing probable cause determinations.[v] Still, *Gerstein* and *Riverside* seemed focused on preventing significant restraints on liberty for those accused and not convicted of crimes.

The Court's 1987 decision in *U.S. v. Salerno* struck a different chord, however. The decision is best described as a *Jedi mind trick,* an intellectually dishonest opinion that infinitely changed the way we, as a society, view punishment, and not for the better. The decision upheld, for the first time in history, a measure that would result in the preemptive detention of an individual for crimes he *might* commit upon release. The Court held that the Act did not violate constitutional principles against pre-conviction punishment because it served a legitimate regulatory goal of public safety.

In an impassioned dissent, the late Justice Thurgood Marshall likened the decision to the "tyranny and the excesses of a police state," which the founders deemed "incompatible with the fundamental human rights protected by our Constitution."[vi] He explained that the distinction the majority had crafted between incarceration for regulatory purposes and incarceration for punitive purposes was a joke. He wrote:

> The majority concludes that the Act is a regulatory rather than a punitive measure . . . that "Congress did not formulate the pretrial detention provisions as punishment for dangerous individuals," but instead was pursuing the "legitimate regulatory goal" of "preventing danger to the community" . . . the ease with which the conclusion is reached suggests the worthlessness of the achievement.

Justice Marshall was spot on. The distinction between regulatory and penal when it comes to any period of incarceration is a legal fiction. As a practical matter, it is impossible for jail and prison to be seen as anything but penal, regardless of whether incarceration is experienced pretrial or post-conviction. To be sure, the fact that I was held for eighteen hours while my paperwork was processed did not make my time in jail any more pleasurable or any less punitive. Similarly, the fact that *Salerno* and its progeny suggest that pretrial detention is regulatory in purpose does not make the decision to detain the accused any less of a restraint on liberty. Yet, too often, prosecutors' offices encourage line attorneys to request detention simply because there is a statutory basis through which to do so. Pre-trial detention has evolved into a "CYA" mechanism. God forbid, we decline to seek detention in a case, and the accused re-offends on release. Covering ourselves has become more important than sensible, individualized treatment that acknowledges the significant restraint and harm caused by incarceration.

When a prosecutor recognizes the significance of any liberty restraint, regardless of when during the criminal process it is imposed, he behaves differently. He does not request detention simply because he can, or to impose pressure on the accused to submit to a plea. When a prosecutor views the liberty interest of the accused as significantly as she views her own, she pushes back when told to seek detention simply because the law allows. She takes the time to make well-reasoned, individualized decisions, recognizing that another human being's liberty interest is at stake. She encourages her police officer colleagues to issue citations and desk appearance tickets (DATs) where no legitimate law enforcement purpose is served by detention, even for one night.

In some jurisdictions, citations and DATs can be issued in lieu of a formal arrest for many misdemeanor and nonviolent offenses. Once the alleged offense falls within the citation or DAT policy, police officers have the discretion to issue these tickets, which instruct the accused to appear in court at a certain date and time, allowing them to skip the trauma of even one night in jail.[vii] New York is one example. There, whenever a police officer determines there is probable cause for an arrest, he also has the option to issue a DAT for most non-violent misdemeanors.[viii] On November 29, 2019, the Arresting Officer could have served me with a DAT. Instead, he exercised his discretion to callously deprive me of my liberty, not because he had to, but because he could; because, as he put it when he visited my jail cell shortly after my arrest, "of [my] mouth." That night, the Arresting Officer did not give a second thought to his decision, or how it would affect my emotional health, physical health, job, future, reputation, income, or family. He chose to have me spend one night in jail, not because I posed a danger to the community, but simply out of spite.

Yet, as painful and traumatizing as the arrest and aftermath have been for me, I am not among the most vulnerable—those who can least afford the consequences of an arrest. I was not in danger of losing my job for one missed day of work, or forfeiting a housing voucher by virtue of a pending criminal case. However, many people are so vulnerable. "Poor people, especially people of color, face a far greater risk of being . . . arrested, and even incarcerated for minor offenses than other Americans."[ix] This fact, known as the "criminalization of poverty," creates further barriers to overcoming poverty by, amongst other things, limiting "access [to] resources that make a safe and decent life possible.[x] The ability of police officers to disrupt life and liberty on a whim ought to be discouraged, and prosecutors are best equipped to challenge such practices. They can start by encouraging the issuance of citations and DATs when the subject of an arrest poses no viable risk to public safety.

Every prosecutor ought to read the *Gerstein*, *Riverside*, and *Salerno* decisions in full to recognize how far we've come and how far we have left to go. Not every hold is worth seeking, simply because we have a statutory basis upon which to do so; not every 911 call, or *malum prohibitum* act, ought to result in a formal arrest, accompanied by a night in jail. In law school, we are taught to read, examine, and challenge. In private practice, we are encouraged to think creatively. When practicing in-house (e.g., inside of a corporation), we are expected to identify novel solutions for complex problems. In prosecution, however, we are trained to regard legislators—who proscribe penalties and procedure in a vacuum—as omniscient, but they are not, and we are not puppets. No two fact patterns are the same and, as prosecutors, we must be able to recognize when the prescriptions of legislators are ill-suited to our particular case.

Where liberty is concerned, prosecutors must be trained to make decisions that take the individual characteristics of the accused into account. Liberty is a fundamental right and any liberty restraint is, in fact, punishment. Each case, each defendant, and each decision affecting liberty is an opportunity to balance and improve the scales of justice.

LESSON 4: THERE IS PUNISHMENT IN THE PROCESS

We often think of punishment in a monolithic way—the way I did when I was a rookie prosecutor. We incorrectly believe punishment begins post-conviction. The reality is that the punishment begins much sooner, regardless of whether the accused is detained, or released on a personal promise to return to court. There is some degree of punishment inherent to being on the other side of the "v."

The most obvious form of pretrial punishment is pretrial detention. In the District of Columbia (D.C.), most individuals are released following their initial appearance, or presentment, except under certain circumstances. The Bail Reform Act, as applied in Washington, D.C., assures release into the community unless the accused has a pending case, is considered a flight risk, or is deemed a danger to a specific person or to the community.

However, detention is not the only factor that makes the process punitive. There is punishment in the process even when the accused is permitted to re-enter the community post-arrest on her promise to abide by conditions set by the court. There is punishment, even in the absence of such conditions, simply by virtue of being subject to a pending case. There is stigma, there is fear, there is anxiety.

The case of Christopher Thompson provides an apt

illustration. The matter involved several young, Black professionals; it was the only trial I ever handled in D.C. Superior Court where my witnesses and the defendant were more educated than many of my jurors. All were college-educated, and many held master's degrees.

Thompson was in his late twenties and this case represented his first arrest. In December 2017, he attended a party. There, he saw a girl. Not just any girl—a baddie. We'll call her Hellen. She was exceptionally pretty with a Coke-bottle body. There was just one problem . . . Hellen had a boyfriend, Mark. At some point during the evening, Mark observed Hellen uncomfortably trying to create space between herself and Thompson. As any boyfriend would, Mark stepped in. Mark was not violent or aggressive, but he was firm. He told Thompson to "fall back" because Hellen and Mark were together.

Believing Thompson had gotten the hint, Mark and Hellen redirected their attention to ordering an Uber so that they could leave the party. But Thompson was not finished. He felt "punked." He was humiliated. Mark had embarrassed him, in front of his friends, on his celebratory graduation weekend, no less. Thompson was furious. So he picked up a Hennessey bottle, charged across the room, and broke that bottle over Mark's face—breaking Mark's nose and orbital bone, causing him to lose consciousness, and causing permanent numbness to his scalp, as well as a scar. But that was not all.

Shards of glass flew across the room with such velocity that they struck a young woman, Mary, who happened to be Mark's best friend. Mary also lost consciousness and, moreover, experienced extreme emotional trauma. Her trauma was unmistakable during her testimony at trial, and also at sentencing when she delivered her victim impact statement to the court.

Once Thompson turned himself in, he was charged with aggravated assault while armed, and assault with significant bodily injury while armed. As a result of one split-second, impulsive decision, a young man with no criminal record now faced five-and-a-half to fifteen years in prison, if convicted of both offenses. It was a difficult case, not due to factual complexity, but because the punishment outlined by statute, and by the D.C. Sentencing Commission, seemed far in excess of any risk that Thompson continued to pose to the community—apart from one poor, alcohol-induced decision made on that December night.

The case was assigned to me approximately one month before trial, and there was a lot to do. I learned that Thompson was represented by Ryan McMann. I knew Mr. McMann's name and face, but I had not worked with him before the Thompson case. I was warned that he was theatrical and animated, which did not concern me. I was more than comfortable being "the show." In other words, there was nothing boring or mundane about my own trial presentation. Quite the contrary: trial was my element. I recall pleading with Mr. McMann to convince Thompson to take a plea to a lesser offense that would likely result in probation, given his lack of criminal history. However, Thompson was afraid that any felony charge would cost him his job. I pleaded:

> But Ryan, the government's case is strong. He may lose his job either way; but does he also want to lose his freedom? What is he going to do, claim Mark had a knife?

As it turned out, that was exactly what the defense intended to do.

I remember it like it was yesterday. I can vividly recall the moment McMann stood before the jury and asserted that Mark, the victim, instigated the incident by approaching Thompson with a knife. I was livid. Thompson had now victimized Mark not once, but twice. While I would happily have a cup of coffee with Mr. McMann today, back then, I was more inclined to throw one at him. I cringed while listening to witness after witness for the defense re-victimize Mark, this time with an assault on his character. In the end, the jury did not buy it. Thompson was convicted on both counts, indicating that the jury had rejected his untenable self-defense claim. Now, Thompson—a young man who had never so much as been arrested before this case— faced real jail time. I wanted justice for the victims, but five-and-a-half to fifteen years was not it.

By the time of Thompson's sentencing, I was a few months past my own arrest, and still on "desk duty"—a regulatory measure, for sure, that nonetheless felt like punishment. I remember drafting the sentencing memorandum and scouring the sentencing guidelines for a "mitigating factor" to undercut Thompson's culpability and thus exposure. I found none. Thompson's only redeeming quality was that he was a first-time offender—a factor accounted for by his guidelines range, and not a basis for seeking a downward departure (e.g., a lower period of incarceration). The fact was that Thompson had done a terrible thing and then lied about it. Still, five-and-a-half to fifteen years did not feel like justice.

My supervisors disagreed. They advised me to seek a guidelines-compliant sentence without further specification, and to let the judge decide. It was a "cover your ass" measure designed to protect the office should the defendant re-offend, a decision that presumes the D.C. Sentencing Commission got it right, and that punishment begins post-conviction. The reality is that the punitive nature of a criminal contact begins with arrest. As I listened to Mr. McMann convey this point at sentencing, I could not help but see the parallels between Thompson and me:

I think what sometimes is lost, Your Honor, is the fact

that the stress and anxiety that comes along with not knowing what's going to happen, not knowing what this Court is going to do in terms of sentencing, and then not knowing how that sentence is going to affect the rest of one's life is meaningful. It's punishment. And I ask the Court to consider the fact that this young man has been in this posture for a significant period of time. Each time I've spoken with him, while I've tried to have him go through this process with the least amount of anxiety as possible, I can tell that it weighs heavy; it weighs heavy upon him, as it does right now.

I listened to these words, not from counsel's table, but from the gallery of the courtroom, while my former supervisor handled the sentencing. Why? Because there is punishment in the process.

That punishment precluded me from appearing on the record in Court, on behalf of the United States, while pending criminal charges in New York City. I had poured my heart into Thompson's case to prepare for trial, in pursuit of justice for Mark and Mary. I secured witnesses from other jurisdictions. When I learned that crime scene investigators failed to report to the scene to secure physical evidence, I found photos of the inside of the home where the assault occurred on the internet. I worked with the U.S. military to secure a witness who sought to use military service as a shield against the government's subpoena power. I used personal funds to procure trial demonstratives—such as a Hennessy bottle and a porcelain human skull. And after the defense's fabricated self-defense testimony, I spent the weekend before closing arguments securing a witness whose testimony confirmed that Mark neither possessed nor brandished a knife; a witness who could describe in detail the way in which Thompson charged toward Mark, unprovoked, with Hennessy bottle in hand, and cracked that bottle open over Mark's face. Yet there I was, watching someone else take the role of lead counsel, in *my* case, at sentencing—one of the most important proceedings of the criminal justice process.

Part of my "punishment" included uncertainty. I would be relegated to "desk duty" in a section where I would be asked to work on cases I deemed uninspiring at best, and unjust at worst. I would live in a state of purgatory, not knowing how one night would affect the rest of my life. It was punishment, and like Mr. McMann said, it weighed heavily on me, in that moment and in every moment since that November night, to this day. By the time of Thompson's sentencing, I had been in that posture for two months. Thompson had been in that posture for two years.

The judge appeared to agree that Thompson had suffered enough. She elected not to follow the sentencing guidelines in that case, and sentenced Thompson to probation. Before my colleague and I left the courthouse, Thompson thanked us, but any debt he owed was to the judge. The judge recognized that a one-size-fits-all approach is better reserved for clothing than for criminal cases. She understood that sometimes the sentencing guidelines and the legislature get it wrong; she acknowledged that justice does not always demand jail-time, and sometimes incarceration does more harm than good. She came to this conclusion by considering more than the conduct proven; she considered the person before her. The person she'd observed in countless hearings, his history, his present, and his prospective future. And she made a decision to exercise her discretion in a way that considered the humanity of the individual standing before her.

I cannot say that I completely agree with the judge's

decision to suspend all of Thompson's sentence—especially given the permanent injuries that Mark sustained, Mary's trauma, and Mary's request that Thompson serve some period of incarceration. However, the judge's decision creates a ripe opportunity for discourse on mercy, empathy, and humanity in criminal justice outcomes; the type of mercy we often see dispensed in favor of the rich (often White), educated, and politically connected. In this particular case, Thompson—a young Black man—benefited from the system's education bias. It was clear as early as the defense's opening, that Thompson and McMann intended to exploit Thompson's credentials and accomplishments at trial. Although their strategy did not work on the jury, I am not sure I can say the same for the judge. I often wonder whether the judge would have been as inclined to show Thompson grace had he not been a master's recipient, perceived as having a promising future.

I encourage you to consider the impact of education and other indications of status as you read the chapters that follow. While no two cases permit a precise 1:1 comparison—each involving its own unique facts and characters; class, wealth, and connections continue to impact how we perceive the accused, his ability to be rehabilitated, and his worthiness of redemption. I submit to you that as long as these class-related considerations continue to affect how the accused fares in the halls of justice, we cannot credibly reject considering those factors over which the accused arguably has less control.

LESSON 5: CONSIDER THE PERSON; NOT JUST THE CONDUCT

The way our system is currently set up, sentencing usually provides the first opportunity for the prosecutor to learn about the person on the other side of the "v." Prior to that point, the prosecutor only knows what the investigation reveals. That knowledge generally includes police reports, witness statements, forensic evidence, and other material used to assess probable cause and the overall strength of the case. However, it is unlikely that the prosecutor knows anything about the accused beyond age, race, gender, and the conduct alleged.

It is not until weeks after a conviction by trial or guilty plea that the prosecutor receives substantive information about the person charged. This information is provided in the form of a Pre-Sentence Report (PSR). The initial sections of the PSR identify and describe the accused, explain the charged conduct, present the facts underlying the charges at issue, and provide the accused's criminal history score. But there is more.

In a section generally referred to as "Offender Characteristics," the prosecutor learns of the offender's place of birth, parentage, and the circumstances of his rearing. She learns whether the offender experienced abuse or neglect as a child, and whether the offender suffers from mental or physical health deficits. The report offers in-depth information concerning the accused's history of drug abuse or addiction, as well as educational, vocational, and employment history. Finally, the PSR offers insight into the financial affairs of the accused, who—in most violent crime cases—does not have so much as a credit card to his name.

In short, the PSR provides the prosecutor with valuable information concerning the person charged, and offers insight into how the accused landed on the other side of the "v." It is not uncommon for prosecutors to review the PSR and be overwhelmed by the life experience, trauma, and history of the accused. Such information would, in many cases, impact the exercise of prosecutorial discretion from indictment to plea-bargaining, and every stage in between. Yet our system is deliberately structured to eliminate empathy from the calculus, until sentencing.

The PSR was created to add value to the criminal justice process by permitting individualized treatment of the defendant and his specific case. A 1973 Fordham Urban Law Journal article describes the theory behind the PSR:

> In theory the pre-sentencing report, by individualizing the defendant and his case, assists the judge in assessing what the deterrent, retributive or rehabilitative effect on the defendant would be and thus helps [the judge] to select the appropriate sentence [or punishment].[i]

While sentencing is reserved for the tail end of the criminal justice process, you now know that punishment is not. Punishment, in a real sense, is inherent to any arrest, any period of detention, and any pending case. Receiving the PSR and the information it offers at the tail end of the process is counterintuitive, when it can, and should, impact more than just the government's sentencing request or allocution. Such information has the power and ability to affect a prosecutor's entire approach to the case. Thus, it is worth asking why individualized treatment of the defendant should not occur long before sentencing.

It is unlikely that our entire system will shift to a practice wherein fulsome reports are available at the beginning of a case. But that does not mean that a prosecutor is without means to understand the person she is prosecuting by opening the lines of communication with defense counsel, and even gaining access to previously prepared PSRs when they are available. Knowledge concerning the person being prosecuted impacts every decision the prosecutor makes, because it affects how the prosecutor views the accused.

Consider *United States v. Alexander Jones,* a case I inherited as a felony assistant in the domestic violence trial unit. The system failed Mr. Jones in nearly every conceivable way by responding to the conduct without consideration of the person.

Jones was almost thirty years old when he became entangled in the criminal justice system for the first time. On September 3, 2017, he crashed his girlfriend's car at the intersection of 12th and Pennsylvania Avenue N.W. in Washington, D.C.—concluding a police chase that began in the northeast quadrant of the city. The crash was the climax of a multi-day-long feud between Jones and his girlfriend, Ruby. Jones had taken Ruby's car from her Maryland home days earlier without her permission. He then lured her into D.C. to meet him with the promise of returning her car. Once they met, it became clear to Jones that Ruby had no desire to reconcile. Jones had been drinking and refused to return Ruby's car keys. Desperate to regain possession of her car, Ruby jumped into the back seat of the car before Jones could get away.

It got worse. Jones, while driving erratically, pulled a knife out of his sock and held it toward Ruby. The initial investigation suggested that Jones may have tried to harm Ruby with the knife, but that fact was not clearly established at trial. Fearful for her life, Ruby jumped out of the moving car. She used a bystander's cell phone to report the incident, including vehicular theft. When a license plate reader in the district detected the location of the vehicle, officers initiated a traffic stop, but Jones had other plans. A chase ensued, resulting in Jones pinning an officer between the door and body of a squad car and striking two other vehicles before ultimately crashing into a vehicle occupied by a mother and her two young children.

Without question, the facts were bad. In a very short period of time, Jones had made a multitude of bad decisions and racked up a series of serious felony charges. And, if Jones was only the sum of his worst decisions, then yes, he had earned the decades of jail time he now faced. But there was *gray*.

There was more to the story. Days before the incident, Ruby had given birth to their severely premature baby. Concerned about his child's chances of survival, Jones had defaulted to self-medicating with drugs and alcohol. Not helping his case, he had assaulted Ruby at least once during this period by striking her in the face—the act that set into motion the events leading up to his arrest. Still, Jones had no history of violence. His only prior criminal contacts included four-year-old convictions for drunk driving offenses and disruptive behavior. It did not take a rocket scientist to realize that Mr. Jones's problems might be related to his substance abuse.

By any standard, Jones broke the law, and his abuse of Ruby, his postpartum partner, was unjustifiable. Jones was also dealing with significant life stresses without appropriate coping mechanisms. Both of these things can be true at the same time, and should have been considered when fashioning release conditions and extending a plea offer. But they were not. The only factors considered were Jones's conduct over that very short period of time, and the penalties associated with the offenses with which he was charged. As a result, Jones was not released after his arrest, nor was he released at any time while pending trial. He remained in Department of Corrections custody from the time of his arrest, and was remanded to the Bureau of Prisons to complete his sentence post-conviction.

Here are just a few ways in which the system failed Jones. First, Jones did not have competent counsel until sentencing. There is no way that Jones should have been held pending trial in lieu of requiring inpatient drug and alcohol treatment. Upon completion of such a program, a judge likely could have fashioned conditions to ensure Jones's continued appearance in court and the safety of the community—in this case, Ruby. At the very least, he could have been held initially, but released on a motion to modify conditions prior to trial. No attorney assigned to his case made such a pre-trial motion.

The D.C. Public Defender Service (PDS), reputed to be one of the best in the nation, was conflicted off of Jones's case because the bystander, whose phone Ruby used to report the incident, was a PDS attorney and a witness in the investigation and at trial. I recall my predecessor being pleased that PDS was conflicted off of the case because "they would have made our jobs much more difficult." There is no doubt in my mind that Jones would have been released pending trial had he been represented by PDS. So the first way the system failed Jones was in its appointment of representation.

The second way the system failed Jones was at the plea-negotiation stage. By the time I inherited the case, a plea offer of seven years had already been extended and rejected. My predecessor and his supervisors viewed seven years as reasonable, despite Jones's lack of criminal history, because under the relevant statutes and sentencing guidelines, Jones's exposure was much more severe. They offered seven years' incarceration to a man who had never before committed any act of violence and who, up until that point, had never spent more than a night or two behind bars. It is no wonder that Jones elected to take his chances and go to trial.

I offered a new plea post-indictment, immediately before the trial. I obtained approval to restructure the original offer so that a significant portion of the time served would be suspended. In other words, Jones would serve some of the time right away and, upon his release, if he did not re-offend within the allotted probationary period, the suspended time would expire. However, my hands were tied given the severity of the initial offer. Supervisors rarely approve a post-indictment plea offer that is more lenient than the one offered pre-indictment. So I tried, but I could not get approval for anything likely to sway Jones from risking the exposure he would face if convicted at trial.

The trial of Mr. Jones presented one of my gravest bouts of cognitive dissonance. I knew that Mr. Jones had made a series of poor, impulsive decisions that threatened and posed risk to the mother of his child, and a number of other people who just happened to be in the wrong place at the wrong time. I had done everything I could to spare Mr. Jones a conviction that would expose him to decades of prison time, because I did not (and do not) believe the penalty prescribed for the offenses charged fit Mr. Jones's case. But by late April 2018, it was clear that we would be taking Mr. Jones to trial. The trial ended with a guilty verdict on several felony counts. Under the guidelines, his total exposure exceeded twenty-five years' incarceration.

At sentencing, we learned that Mr. Jones was not only under the influence of alcohol at the time of the incident, but that he struggled with other substances. At the heart of Mr. Jones's case were untreated drug and alcohol issues. The system's prescribed rehab center was a federal penitentiary.

My colleague and I remained at odds as to what the appropriate sentence should be in Mr. Jones's case. Ultimately, the judge imposed a period of eight years' incarceration, where three of those years would be suspended. It was a more favorable sentence than the pre-indictment offer, further establishing the excessiveness of seven years given Mr. Jones's complete history.

Mr. Jones's case is an apt illustration of how justice fails when we do not consider the *gray*. A comprehensive look at Mr. Jones, his history, and the underlying causes of his conduct at the outset of the case would have resulted in forced drug and alcohol treatment, rather than initial detention. We should have treated the root of Mr. Jones's problems, rather than reacting to their symptoms. Mr. Jones was an excellent candidate for rehabilitation under most metrics; however, he only experienced the retributive facets of the system.

Prosecutors must be trained to ask themselves two fundamental questions at every stage of a case: "What does the law allow me to do, and what should I do to achieve justice for the community and for all of the individuals most affected by this alleged crime?"[ii] I guarantee that when the humanity of the accused is part of the calculus, the answers to those two questions will rarely be the same.

LESSON 6: END COERCIVE PLEA BARGAINING

The extraordinary power of the prosecutor undoubtedly extends to the plea-bargaining process. Statistics show that 95 percent of federal and state criminal matters are resolved by plea.[i] While the process by which a plea is entered into is referred to as a bargain, it has also been described as more akin to "legal extortion," where the accused is heavily pressured to accept deals out of fear of more serious charges and/or more severe penalties.[ii]

There are three commonly used plea tactics that undermine the bargaining aspect and, thus, the fundamental fairness of the process. They include (1) overcharging, (2) conditional plea offers, and (3) phased plea offers.

Overcharging occurs when the prosecutor obtains an indictment on offenses for which there is arguably probable cause, but low probability of obtaining a conviction beyond a reasonable doubt. Michelle Alexander writes that, as a result of this practice, defendants often feel compelled to forfeit their right to a jury trial:

> When prosecutors offer "only" three years in prison, when the penalties defendants could receive if they took their case to trial would be five, ten, or twenty years—or life

imprisonment—only extremely courageous (or foolish) defendants turn the offer down.[iii]

The "conditional plea offer" invites the defendant to forfeit certain rights, or lose the benefit of the more generous early offer. For instance, if the defense believes a charge is meritless, or that a constitutional violation occurred at the time of arrest, a pre-trial motion or hearing is required to bring the issue before a judge. However, many prosecutors "condition" the early offer—which is most often the least punitive offer—on the defendant's waiver of these rights.

Finally, prosecutors frequently engage in "phased" plea offers, similar to that described in relation to Alexander Jones, *supra*. With respect to that process, the most generous offer an accused will ever see is extended shortly after their arrest. The more effort and time extended by the prosecutor and his office, the less generous the offer becomes. For example, a prosecutor may offer a pre-preliminary hearing (PPH) offer. If a PPH offer is rejected, the prosecutor proceeds toward indictment. As the prosecutor nears indictment, he will extend a pre-indictment offer, usually one less generous than the PPH offer. If that offer is rejected, the prosecutor moves forward with indictment. Once a grand jury indicts, the prosecutor will extend a post-indictment offer before significant trial preparation begins.

Inherent to each offer is more exposure, i.e., prison time, and more serious charges than the last. Moreover, once trial preparation begins, all bets are generally off. If the defendant wants to avoid trial at that late stage, you often hear the prosecutor require the accused to "eat the indictment," or plead to all counts.

These and other tactics are antithetical to a fair and balanced plea-bargaining process. The Supreme Court has fully endorsed plea bargaining; however, that endorsement "presupposes fairness in securing the agreement."[iv] Currently, the plea-bargaining process seems more geared toward caseload management than fair outcomes. Prosecutors must be taught to resist the urge to overcharge, and coercive plea-bargaining tactics must be discouraged.

Resist the Impulse to Overcharge

In 2017, the DOJ issued a memorandum on the Department Charging and Sentencing Policy. The policy encouraged prosecutors to "charge and pursue the most serious, readily provable offense." The directive expressly superseded a prior directive, issued by former Attorney General Eric Holder, discouraging the use of offenses carrying mandatory minimum penalties.[v] What is much less cited, however, is the express recognition in the 2017 memorandum that "[t]here will be circumstances in which good judgment would lead a prosecutor to conclude that a strict application of the above charging policy is not warranted."

While many government attorneys view the 2017 memorandum as exacerbating the mass incarceration crisis (and it certainly does), and undermining line-prosecutor discretion (it does that too); it also invites the line prosecutor to use her voice and good judgment to argue against "strict application" of the policy when it is deemed ill-suited for a particular case. In such instances, the line-prosecutor should, in theory, feel empowered to push back against the pressure to charge the most serious, readily provable offense, particularly when optics or the *gray* so require.

For example, imagine an instance where a firearm is recovered from a home in Washington, D.C., and fingerprint analysis leads to a suspect. The suspect does not reside at the home, but has been seen entering the location from time to time. Further, as a result of the suspect's criminal history, and the fact that no firearms are manufactured in the District of Columbia, the prosecutor *may* seek to charge the suspect with Felon-in-Possession ("FIP") under the federal criminal code. Indeed, many would consider FIP to be the "most readily provable offense" on these facts. But optically, should a prosecutor move forward with such a case?

I submit that presenting this particular case to a grand jury would constitute classic overreaching given the limited value of fingerprint evidence on these facts. In the event the prosecutor was able to secure an indictment, he might offer a plea to a lessor charge or agree to limit the accused's exposure, thereby "extorting" a plea on facts that could hardly be proven beyond a reasonable doubt at trial.

Overcharing, which includes overreaching, directly hurts the credibility of the prosecutor, their office, and the system as a whole. Prosecutors must be strongly discouraged from indicting on tenuous charges as a scare tactic to secure a plea. A case is generally as strong as it will ever be on the date of indictment. If you doubt your ability to prove any charge beyond a reasonable doubt on the day of indictment, that charge should not be presented to the grand jury.

Discontinue Coercive Plea Bargaining

There is no better way to understand the difference between fair and coercive plea-bargaining than to consider how you would want to be treated if you were the person on the other side of the "v." How responsive would you hope the assigned prosecutor would be? How much discovery or evidence would you want to have, and within what time frame? Would you want to have all relevant and material items of evidence before you made a decision that would affect the next several months or years of your life? Would you want to be pressured to accept an early offer out of fear that your exposure would only increase? Would you want your offer conditioned on whether or not you challenged unconstitutional acts by the police? Yet, these are tactics routinely employed by prosecutors that go virtually unchallenged.

The practice of conditioning plea offers on the accused waiving a probable cause hearing is oppressive. The practice of withdrawing the offer, should the defendant file an affirmative motion, is appalling. The decision to up the ante on a defendant's exposure as the case progresses through phased plea bargaining is, as Howard describes it, akin to "legal extortion."[vi] If a plea offer is fair on a set of facts at the outset of a case, it is fair up until the day of trial, absent new, material information about the conduct alleged. It does not matter how much time the prosecutor spends preparing for trial, responding to motions, or drafting case impression memoranda in preparation for an indictment. That is the job.

While many systemic issues are difficult to fix as a line prosecutor, all prosecutors can choose to employ fair, humane plea-negotiation tactics now. Do unto the accused as you would like done unto you should you one day—as far-fetched as it may sound—find yourself on the other side of the "v."

LESSON 7: REJECT THE "BRADY BURDEN" MINDSET

The term *Brady* in prosecutors' offices has become a dirty word—one that triggers fear, disdain, and anxiety. The term derives from the Supreme Court's 1963 decision in *United States v. Brady* when two men—Boblit and Brady—were charged with first-degree murder in connection with a robbery they conspired to commit. Boblit confessed to the killing and the two men were tried separately. However, Boblit's confession was not disclosed to Brady until after Brady was tried, convicted, and sentenced to death.

Based on these facts, the Supreme Court held that "the suppression by the prosecution of evidence favorable to an accused upon request violates due process when the evidence is material, either to guilt or to punishment, irrespective of the good faith or bad faith of the prosecution."[i] The core principle underlying the decision was as follows:

> Society wins, not only when the guilty are convicted, but when criminal trials are fair; our system of the administration of justice suffers when any accused is treated unfairly ... a prosecution that withholds evidence on demand of an accused which, if made available, would tend to exculpate him, or reduce the penalty, helps shape

a trial that bears heavily on the defendant. That casts the prosecutor in the role of an architect of a proceeding that does not comport with standards of justice.[ii]

It speaks volumes that there even had to be a *Brady* decision when, almost two decades prior, the Court recognized the prosecutor as no "ordinary party to a controversy," and one whose mission is to "govern impartially" and fairly in order to ensure that "justice is done."[iii]

As a result of the *Brady* decision, a request for *Brady* evidence is generally included in every request for discovery or evidence by the defense. The prompt disclosure of *Brady* evidence is so important that judges often issue standard *Brady* orders post-indictment, just in case the defense attorney is asleep at the wheel. Disclosure of *Brady* evidence is so crucial that the court will address and remedy the violation, whether the failure to disclose is unintentional or "the result of guile."[iv]

Brady evidence, at the trial phase, is often described as anything that tends to negate the guilt of the accused. It need not be a smoking gun. *Brady* could be contradictions between the accounts of two eyewitnesses; it could be the presence of an unknown fingerprint or specimen of DNA on the weapon used to commit the crime; it could involve a decade-old finding by a judge that undercuts the credibility of a witness; or, in the case of *Brady*, material that mitigates punishment. As AUSAs in Washington, D.C., we were taught to think of *Brady* evidence as anything we would expect the defense would want to know. Still, prosecutors struggle with the term *Brady*; some prosecutors are even considered to have "*Brady* blind spots." According to an article published by the National Association of Defense Lawyers:

[Sixteen] percent of reversals of capital convictions in the

United States from 1973 to 1995 were due to prosecutorial suppression of favorable evidence. In addition, a 2010 Innocence Project study concluded that 10 percent of the 255 DNA exonerations involved allegations on appeal or in civil suits of prosecutorial suppression of evidence.[v]

A scathing 2018 article described a pervasive "willingness to hide evidence to win"[vi] by prosecutors in my former office. The article provided several case examples of egregious *Brady* violations by D.C. AUSAs, commenting that flagrant disregard for the *Brady* rule was simply "business as usual" in USAO-D.C. Such reports should beg the question, why are *Brady* violations so widespread? Is *Brady* excessively burdensome, do prosecutors lack sufficient training or judgment, or is it something more nefarious? I believe prosecutors simply ought to change the way they perceive the *Brady* rule.

Inside the halls of prosecutors' officers, it is not uncommon to hear venting and complaints about the onerous obligations of *Brady* from line and chief prosecutors alike. I have attended *Brady* trainings where the chief or supervisory prosecutor conducting the training gripes about a new rule or decision that increases prosecutors' *Brady* obligations. Prosecutors' views of *Brady*, no doubt, flow from the top down. However, *Brady* obligations are not difficult to honor when prosecutors understand their investigatory function.

In addition to being servants of the law, and no ordinary party to a dispute, prosecutors are investigators. The sole objective of the prosecutor is to uncover the truth. The investigative function of the prosecutor requires that she be so tuned into the facts of a case that she can instantly sense when something is off. She must be able to recognize the most minor of contradictions. Her gut should alert her to any fact that is at odds with an initial or existing theory of the matter she is investigating. She does this not because of *Brady*, but because she is constantly thinking about what makes sense, what rings true, and what a jury will believe.

For example, I once had a case involving the armed robbery of a rideshare driver. The robbery occurred around 2:00 a.m. in Northwest, Washington, D.C. The victim-driver reported that he was parked near several local bars, awaiting "let out" or closing time in hopes of obtaining a fare. While he was parked, the two suspects approached him and requested a ride. They did not have the appropriate rideshare application on their devices, but promised to pay him in cash. He obliged.

If you know anything about Uber, Lyft, and most other rideshares, these facts should strike you as odd. As a frequent user of rideshare services, I was extremely familiar with how these applications work. The rider creates an account that includes personal identifying information, as well as payment information. Once their account information is complete, the rider may request rides through the application. The rideshare application collects data about the rider and the driver—data that provides certain safety assurances for all involved.

For instance, had the victim in my case been robbed or assaulted by a rider assigned through the rideshare application, there would have been a trail of data that could be used to identify a suspect—if not a name, perhaps an email address, credit card number, device identifier (e.g., IMEI), or IP address. For these reasons, it was and is highly unusual for a rideshare driver to operate as a traditional taxi driver, accepting cash for services rather than accepting fares directly through the app.

So why would the driver agree to provide taxi services to two men at an obscene hour by means other than through the application? I probed the complainant and he provided an explanation, but my concerns were not assuaged. His explanations rang hollow. My investigative senses could see right through them, and if I could, so would a jury.

When something does not make sense, consider it a sign that additional investigation is needed. Sometimes, that investigation leads to *Brady* evidence, but the need to conduct such an investigation should not be viewed as burdensome when it is a quintessential element of the prosecutors' investigatory function. In other words, prosecutors should want to learn facts that go against their theory of the case. Disconfirmed beliefs are a gift and not a curse, and there is no better time to learn these things than during the investigatory phase of a case, before a jury is sworn in, and before the liberty interest of the accused is irreversibly restrained.

There are hundreds, maybe even thousands, of cases and studies concerning the prosecutor's *Brady* obligations. The detail and analysis included in these opinions and articles suggest that there is something difficult or complex about satisfying the *Brady* rule, but there is nothing complex about it at all. A shift in mindset is all that is needed, and such a shift can be accomplished without placing witnesses, including victims, at risk.

The safety and security of witnesses is paramount in prosecutors' offices, as it should be. The community cannot be expected to trust and cooperate with the prosecution if prosecutors, and their law enforcement partners, cannot be counted on for protection. When *Brady* evidence raises legitimate security concerns, the Court is the prosecutor's first line of defense. It is the job of judges, not prosecutors, to "balance the reality of potentially life-threatening dangers" to witnesses and their families, with the constitutional right of the accused to prepare a defense.[vii] Barring witness security concerns, prosecutors must recognize that, when it comes to *Brady*, the interests of the prosecution and the defense are aligned. When a prosecutor sees herself as a servant of the law, as described by

Justice Sutherland in *Berger*, she does not see *Brady* as a burden. She sees it as a duty—the satisfaction of which benefits the accused, the government's case, and the integrity of criminal justice as a whole.

LESSON 8: DEFENSE ATTORNEYS ARE OUR FRIENDS

I was less than one week out of basic training when I learned how important it is to develop a relationship and reputation of trust with the defense.

I was assigned to the Misdemeanor Domestic Violence (MDV) trial docket. Back then we received case assignments in bulk, usually fifteen at a time. Our pretrial interaction with the victim usually consisted of a few phone calls. It was rare to meet a victim, or a complainant, before the day of trial. So when I met Marline McCoy, the victim in a newly filed MDV case, while covering arraignments, it was an easy lift to convince my supervisor to reassign Marline's case to me.

The case involved a physical dispute between Marline and her mother-in-law. The two shared a residence and, as a result, the case was accepted by our DV branch. I met Marline less than twenty-four hours after she was assaulted, and the evidence of a physical altercation was all over her face. Despite being inexperienced, I had the presence of mind to take multiple photographs of her injuries.

I was also able to give Marline an in-person rendition of the spiel we were trained to give as MDV prosecutors, which went something like this:

My name is Bianca Forde. I will be the prosecutor on your case. I am so sorry that this happened to you. Today, the defendant will be released because we do not have statutory authority to hold her. Do you have a safe place to go? Would you like us to request a Stay Away Order?

After addressing these concerns, there was one final point to convey—one that has become known as the *Gregory* warning, arising from a 1966 D.C. Circuit Case. The case cemented the principle that no witness belongs to either side; accordingly, it is improper for the prosecutor to prohibit a witness from speaking to the defense, and vice versa. Despite this prohibition, it had become routine for us to advise witnesses of their right to speak, or not to speak, without violating the *Gregory* rule. We would often say:

You may be contacted by the defense, or an investigator working for the defense. We do not provide your personal information, but they have the ability to obtain it through their own means. It is totally up to you whether you choose to speak with them or not (and here comes the most important part) I cannot and will not advise you either way. I just want to make clear that I am the only person from the government that will contact you from this point going forward; if anyone calls you or visits your home, claiming to be a government investigator, ask to see identification so that you know who you are talking to at all times. Do you understand?

In other words, you can talk to these defense attorneys and investigators if you so choose, but just know, they do not have your best interest at heart. Their sole goal is to keep the defendant out of trouble. *Capiche?* That is what I was taught, and that is what I did with Marline, but that is not how Marline heard it.

Marline conveyed the conversation differently when she spoke with the defense. In her version, I had cautioned her not to speak to the defense at all. And the defense—rather than reaching out to me as a courtesy and an act of professionalism to ascertain what had in fact happened—filed a motion instead. In it, they accused me of violating the D.C. Circuit's guidance in *Gregory*. I was livid, but I was also afraid. There I was, my first week as a prosecutor, already in fear of an attack on my bar license. They had warned us about this in basic training. It was early evidence of the lack of trust between the defense bar and prosecution in D.C.—a lack of trust that grew exponentially as our caseloads became more serious and the criminal exposure faced by the accused more significant. This lack of trust hurts no one more than the individual on the other side of the v.

You cannot always control what happens in your life, but you always have the opportunity to control how you respond to it. The defense had raised an issue implicating my credibility and integrity; thus, my supervisor thought it best that a different AUSA handle the case, and the government's response to their accusation, moving forward. I could have allowed the incident involving Marline to frame the way I viewed every defense attorney that I encountered from that point forward, and I would have had good reason to do so. I could have allowed the experience to breed mistrust and resentment for every member of the defense bar—expecting each of them to view my bar license as a casualty along their path toward achieving an acquittal. Or I could do my part to develop a reputation that would not be susceptible to such elementary, brutish attacks. I chose to do the latter.

While I have never heard a prosecutor admit that her relationship with the defense impacts her (the prosecutor's) handling of a case, I have no doubt that it does. We are humans first and prosecutors second. It is natural for our interactions to be affected by whether our feelings about a thing or person are positive or negative, and the impact can be subtle; as subtle as the amount of time it takes to return a phone call, or respond to an email; or the less subtle difference between simply adhering to the rules of discovery and, alternatively, going above and beyond them. As people, we often bend over backwards for those whom we like, respect, and trust; no amount of professionalism or maturity changes that fact.

So fast-forward to a few years after my case involving Marline. I was now assigned to the office's Major Crimes trial unit, and was asked to investigate an armed robbery in which the victim claimed to have been robbed at gunpoint by two unknown Black men. During their investigation, police obtained video evidence from the gas station where the robbery occurred. The video showed the victim at the ATM and one of the suspects standing behind the victim, holding an object to the victim's back. The object was covered by a plastic bag, so there was no way to know for sure that it was a firearm, but it was clear that the suspect's intent was that the victim would believe the object was, in fact, a gun.

Days after meeting the victim and having him testify in the grand jury, I received a call from the defense attorney, a respected attorney for the Public Defender's Service in the District of Columbia ("DC PDS"). She got straight to the point, a quality I very much appreciate.

"Look," she said, "We have not had the chance to work together before, but I understand that my colleagues that have worked with you view you as fair." If you know anything about DC PDS, that was quite the compliment. "I've reviewed the video you sent me—is that the only video you have?"

"Yes," I responded. "That's what we received at papering."

"OK," she added, "My investigator is at the gas station

where this all happened, and he says there's more video. I think it will make a difference, if you're the kind of prosecutor I hear that you are."

The video did make a difference. It painted a starkly different picture than that presented by the victim. When I confronted the victim with the new evidence, his explanation was unsatisfactory. Knowing no jury would believe the victim's incredible version of events, and recognizing that the victim had already perjured himself before the grand jury, I obtained permission to close the investigation and seek the defendant's release from jail. Sometimes justice means walking away.

The defendant's attorney thanked me for "hearing her out," for "honoring my commitment" to take the matters she raised seriously, and for promptly petitioning the court for the defendant's release. On a phone call she mentioned that, but for my reputation, she would have saved the evidence for use at trial to impeach the victim—which would have been less than ideal for all parties, but especially for the defendant, who would have been needlessly detained in D.C. jail up until such time.

Prosecutors must value the role of the defense lawyer, and work towards building relationships and reputations of trust. If you have failed to do so thus far, start now. If you have never valued the role of your adversary, recognize that zealous and talented defense attorneys keep the system balanced and fair. Prosecutors should never celebrate the appointment of incompetence at the defense table. Nor should chief prosecutors portray the defense as thorns in our side that are simply out to get the prosecutor's bar card. Instead, ask what systemic practices prosecutors' offices have been rumored and proven to engage in for ages that have bred these extreme levels of distrust. Then do your best, with your actions, and through the handling of your cases, to change that narrative.

LESSON 9: LET THE GRAY BE YOUR GUIDE

District Court, the venue for federal cases, was initially intimidating. The courtrooms were more traditional and formal than those in Superior Court. Advocates were required to address the judge from a podium, rather than counsel's table. The judges, at least on first glance, were more reserved and stoic. It was as important to learn the judges' quirks as it was to study a whole new set of rules and statutory provisions. The thought of making a mistake was unnerving. I was more anxious than I had ever been in Superior Court, and this anxiety caused me to silence myself in the case of Sherwin Hood, who was before the court for a probation hearing.

Hood had already served eight years in prison following a conviction for distribution of cocaine, while armed and in a school zone, in 2007. It was 2019, and Hood was still under court supervision for the 2007 conviction. Moreover, a judge would now decide whether Hood would return to jail for violating the terms of his post-release supervision. As a condition of his supervision, Hood was required to meet with his probation officer regularly. He now faced four to twelve months in jail for failing to do so—that is, up to one year of incarceration for three technical violations that did not involve a new crime. It was the moment I realized just how unforgiving the U.S. Sentencing

Guidelines could be.

Having read up on Hood's history, I knew he was not a good candidate for probation. His probation had been revoked to incarceration at least twice before, and it seemed appropriate to ask that the court revoke it one last time without implementing any additional period of supervised release. It was, after all, these compounding periods of supervised release that kept Hood perpetually wedded to the system.

Once the hearing began, the judge turned to me to inquire about the government's position. Back in Superior Court, I often requested that the Court permit the defense to speak first. Hearing the defendant's explanation for lack of compliance could, at times, alter the way I chose to proceed. But I was new to District Court practice, and I opted not to disrupt the judge's flow, especially since this particular judge was rumored to be quite gruff.

The defense attorney spoke after me, generally conceding that the defendant's violations exposed him to a four-month period of incarceration for each violation. Finally, we heard from the defendant himself. As he advanced his position, it was readily apparent that he was frustrated and fed up with a system that was either oblivious or indifferent to his life, his experience, and the realities of re-entering society after serving a lengthy prison sentence. He expressed confusion as to why he was being sent back to jail when he had not re-offended. He pleaded with the court that he had secured a job and, if he was sent back to prison, he would be terminated. He explained that he had fallen out of compliance because of continued bouts of homelessness, but the judge showed no empathy.

The judge imposed six months' incarceration, followed by two months in a halfway house and an additional eighteen months of supervised release. I wanted to interject. I wanted to say, "Your Honor, the government changes its position." But

I held my tongue. I convinced myself that it would not have made a difference; after all, the judge had already exceeded my sentencing recommendation. The judge was much more familiar with this defendant's history than me, for sure. And so, I sat at counsel's table, listening to the defendant emotionally plead for a new judge and demand that his case be transferred to another jurisdiction—as the marshals approached the podium to take him into custody.

I do not have many regrets in life; but not speaking up for Mr. Hood is one of them. For weeks, I replayed my failure to use my voice on Hood's behalf. I wondered why I had been so moved by his pleas and so disappointed in myself as an advocate. Hood was not the most sympathetic of defendants, by any means. While this particular probation violation was merely technical, he had been found to violate the substantive terms of his probation on multiple occasions. One of those violations included a conviction for shooting his own brother in the shoulder while on supervised release.

After reading Alexander's *The New Jim Crow: Mass Incarceration in the Age of Colorblindness,* I instantly realized why Hood's case had such an impact on me. If mass incarceration presents the modern-day civil rights challenge, Hood belongs to the class of individuals for whom today's civil rights warriors must fight. The old movement relied on people of impeccable character to garner attention, empathy, and action; today's movement is messy, and the hands of those it holds are less clean. According to Alexander:

> We can continue to ignore those labeled criminals . . . and focus public attention on more attractive plaintiffs—like innocent doctors and lawyers, stopped and searched on freeways [e.g., like me] . . . but if we do so, we should labor under no illusions that we will end mass incarceration,

or shake the foundations of the current racial order . . . we must face the realities of the new caste system and embrace those who are most oppressed by it, if we hope to end the new Jim Crow.[i]

The regret I experienced in Hood's case motivated me to never again abdicate my duty to speak. It reminded me that, as a prosecutor, the crux of my value rested in having the courage to use my voice to achieve justice, even when doing so could result in consequences or, in the words of the late, great, and honorable John Lewis, "good trouble." I have no doubt that my regret following Hood's case affected the zeal with which I advocated for Joseph on that New York City freeway a few weeks later.

Hood appealed the court's ruling and won, except regarding his request for a new judge. The case was remanded back to the same surly District Court judge, and I had a second opportunity to use my voice, but it was not without cost. It was not without cost to Hood, who spent sixty days incarcerated while his case moved through the relevant judicial channels. It was not without Hood likely losing the job he secured before being re-sentenced.

Hood's case represented a pivotal moment in my career as a prosecutor. It made me realize that once a prosecutor is able to see the *gray*, she cannot easily disregard it—at least not without consequence to her conscience. The *gray* becomes the compass that guides our way; and if we ignore its direction once, we are loathed to do so a second time. Teaching the *gray* is the best way to make justice consistent. Prosecuting with the *gray* in mind is the key to dismantling racially disproportionate and mass-incarceration.

LESSON 10: A PATH TOWARD DECARCERATION

Incarceration has become the default in the United States of America. High fives and congratulatory remarks are exchanged amongst prosecutors when a severe sentence is imposed. Press releases are published to alert the public that our offices are tough on crime. And head prosecutors reject sensible decarceral efforts, purportedly on behalf of victims, without citing any data related to what victims want or need. It is no surprise that we have a mass incarceration problem. Nevertheless, it is important for society and prosecutors to recognize that we were not always this way.

In 1972, our combined prison and jail population approximated 330,000. The present-day count is closer to 2.2 million.[i] This rise in incarceration does not directly correlate to an increase in criminal activity. Instead, it is more directly attributed to policy changes advanced under "tough on crime" rhetoric. These policies include mandatory minimums that require judges to sentence offenders to no less than a certain period of incarceration; "truth in sentencing" laws enacted nationwide, requiring offenders to serve at least 80 percent of their sentences, irrespective of evidence of rehabilitation; and the "three strike rule," which too often results in life sentences for nonviolent offenders who face the court for a third time.

As a result of these policies, our prison growth far outpaces our overall population growth,[ii] and the U.S. is now considered a "world leader in the use of imprisonment"[iii]—a title that should give us grave pause, and cause us shame.

Without question, prosecutors have contributed to the mass incarceration crisis. We seek pretrial holds because we have statutory authority to do so, without sufficient focus on the individual characteristics of the accused. We charge offenses that permit lengthy pretrial detention, and nevertheless request that the clock on pretrial detention be tolled or paused while the accused sits in jail considering our plea offer. We ask for the maximum sentence permissible under the guidelines because we expect the judge to simply "split the baby" or impose a prison term smack in the middle of what the defense and government request. We do these things because we assume that the legislature got it right. We assume that just because a series of acts fits within the statutory definition of a crime, or meets the elements of an offense, the assigned penalty is appropriate. But a one-size-fits-all approach is best reserved for T-shirts and baseball caps, not crimes.

The best example of how one size does not fit all when charging a criminal offense is the case of William Gadey. On a Friday night in January 2017, Gadey approached the complainant, a food delivery person en route to deliver an order. Gadey followed the complainant to his car, assaulted him, and robbed him of the food he carried.

The complainant called 911 to report the incident and provided a description and last known location of the suspect. Within minutes, police stopped Gadey approximately two blocks from the offense location. He was carrying the spoils of the robbery—a bag full of Burger King that matched the order picked up by the complainant minutes before. Within the hour, the complainant identified Gadey as his assailant and the contents of the Burger King bag as the stolen property.

Gadey was ultimately tried and convicted of Assault with Intent to Commit Robbery (AWIR)[iv]—a charge that carries a penalty of two to fifteen years in prison.[v] Based on his criminal history score, Gadey's sentencing exposure was 2½ to 6 years in jail. At sentencing, the defense and I were on the same page, and generally agreed to a period of incarceration towards the bottom or low-end of the guidelines. The sentencing judge, however, had a different opinion concerning the danger Gadey posed to the community. She sentenced Gadey to serve 4½ years in prison. Yes, you read that correctly. He was sentenced to 4½ years for snatching a bag of Burger King and smacking someone in the face.

I do not mean to belittle the harm and trauma suffered by the victim. The complainant in Gadey's case was, for sure, deserving of justice. The incident was traumatic and no one deserves to be victimized in that way. Still, one must ask whether a 4½-year sentence was excessive. Certainly, Gadey's conduct fit the statutory definition of AWIR; however, the very fact that the AWIR offense is defined and penalized in a statute broadly titled "Assault with Intent to Kill, Rob, or Poison, or to Commit First-Degree Sexual Abuse, Second-Degree Sexual Abuse or Child Sexual Abuse" illustrates why legislative prescriptions should not supplant the knowledge, judgment, and individualized assessment of the prosecutor most familiar with the facts and players in a case.

Had Gadey committed the same offense in Germany or other parts of Europe he would have served much less time, if any at all. Indeed, according to Howard's research, "in Europe most crimes are punished by day fines and suspended sentences, [however] the U.S. has chosen incarceration as its solution."[vi] Rarely do U.S. prosecutors bat an eye upon hearing the facts and outcome of Gadey's case, because it is our norm.

The U.S. approach to punishment is often described as unusually cruel.

In a thoughtful, comparative analysis, Marc Howard explains that the U.S. is "far apart" from other liberal democracies in terms of its approach to sentencing and incarceration. Here in the U.S., lengthy sentences of ten years or more are standard, but that's not so elsewhere.[vii] In fact, incarceration periods of ten to fifteen years are generally the "upper limit of prison terms in Europe."[viii] Although life sentences still exist in parts of Europe, they are meant to communicate the "gravity of the offense to society and the offender, whereas the actual service of the sentence is governed by norms of mercy."[ix] In other words, an individual may be sentenced to life in prison, but may be released once it has been established through rehabilitation or otherwise that life imprisonment no longer serves a legitimate law enforcement purpose.

When raising these realities in prosecutor circles, I am often asked how the recidivism rates in European countries compare to recidivism rates in the U.S. While a country-by-country comparison is difficult due to variations in how recidivism is defined globally,[x] studies on the U.S. approach to incarceration conclude that prison, in fact, "produces slight increases in recidivism" and, moreover, increases criminality in low risk offenders.[xi] Notably, while all countries struggle with preventing the convicted from re-offending upon release to some degree, these challenges have not resulted in the abandonment of rehabilitative efforts.[xii] Howard explains:

> [N]ot only has the concept of rehabilitation neither diminished nor died, but in many European countries the objective has actually been reinvigorated in recent years. .

. . [T]he main priority and primary purpose of prison [in much of Europe] remains to rehabilitate and reintegrate criminals by helping them to develop education and skills that will keep them away from prisons in the future.[xiii]

In stark contrast, the U.S. prison system's focus on punishment to the exclusion of "drug treatment, education, or training programs, [leaves] inmates . . . less prepared to function in normal society upon their eventual release,"[xiv] unsurprisingly increasing the likelihood that they will re-offend.

Prosecutors must recognize that our current approach is not effective.

One of the biggest impediments to change and innovation in prosecutors' offices is the shortsighted belief that the way we have always done it is the best and only way. Marc Mauer, a leading expert on sentencing policy, describes why the "*lock 'em up*" approach is unsound from a public safety perspective. First, offenders "age out" of crime. He adds that lengthy sentences are "particularly ineffective for drug crimes, as drug sellers are easily replaced in the community." Second, higher incarceration penalties do little to deter crime.

Take for instance, the individuals selected for federal gun possession charges by chief prosecutors within the USAO-DC under the FIP-Initiative, discussed in Chapter 16. The increased penalty would not be considered an effective way to deter illegal gun possession. Rationally thinking individuals consider a variety of factors when deciding whether to unlawfully possess a firearm, such as whether to enter public spaces, what type of clothing to wear, and how to behave upon encountering police officers. Mauer argues that these individuals do so:

... to avoid being caught in the act because being arrested and prosecuted will impose significant burdens ... additionally, because the individual is not planning on being apprehended, he is unlikely to be thinking about how much time he might spend in prison, and whether his sentence will be three, five, or seven years.[xv]

Ultimately, because the individual who chooses to unlawfully possess a firearm has no intention of being caught, USAO-DC's decision to expose certain FIP defendants to federal penalties has no deterrent value whatsoever. It merely serves to expose more young men—usually young Black men— to federal convictions where the penalties are far greater, and the supervision periods longer, than they would be under local DC law. When prosecutors stop assuming that the legislature got it right and stop supporting the one-size-fits-all approach to punishment, when they realize that the way we administer justice in the U.S. is neither the only way, nor the best way, only then will they handle their cases in a manner that thoughtfully and morally deals with the mass incarceration crisis.

It is my hope that prosecutors' offices will begin to move into the 21st century, where research and empirical data govern law enforcement responses to crime and punishment; where it is understood that a bias for action over data-driven approaches may curb crime in the short term, but will lead to increased crime and community devastation in the long run. It is time for us, as a society, but particular those in law enforcement, to recognize the dangers inherent to focusing on the symptoms of the problem (e.g., the violence), rather than the root causes (e.g., poverty, poor education, lack of resources). No line prosecutor should begin her service, deputized to take action that affects the liberty of another, without having a thorough grasp of these realities.

LESSON 11: HUMANITY IS PART OF THE JOB DESCRIPTION

In March 2020, I was invited to speak to a class of George Washington University law students. Toward the end of the presentation, I was asked for my perspective on the prosecutor's obligation to counteract the various ways in which the criminal justice system dehumanizes those entangled by it. It was a good question, particularly in the midst of COVID-19—a crisis that unapologetically exposed our indifference to the humanity of the accused and the convicted in a way that could not be ignored.

During the COVID-19 crisis, jails became petri dishes for spreading the contagion. The unsanitary conditions within American jails and prisons, coupled with overcrowding, turned U.S. penal institutions into breeding grounds for transmission. The virus was spreading behind bars at a rate that exponentially outpaced the rate of infection in surrounding communities, and it was widely known that jails and prisons were simply ill-equipped to deal with COVID-19.

As a result, we observed some elected prosecutors, mostly at the state level, taking sensible action. Many placed a moratorium on the prosecution of low-level offenders who posed minimal public safety risk. Some ordered their frontline attorneys to abstain from requesting bail and detention in cases involving nonviolent offenders. Many recommended the release of the most vulnerable members of the prison population, based on age or preexisting health conditions. These responses were needed—and needed quickly—because an outbreak behind bars could prove to be catastrophic. In other words, COVID-19 demanded that we pay attention to and re-evaluate our approach to detention and incarceration. Some prosecutors aggressively took up the mantle; others continued onward, business as usual, because the bodies in American jails and prisons were, in their opinion, discardable. This lack of regard for the incarcerated has always stood in the way of sensible criminal justice reform.

For example, in July 2019, Senators Cory Booker and Karen Bass proposed the Second Look Act of 2019 to "enable incarcerated persons to petition a Federal court for a second look at sentences longer than ten years."[i] The Act provided guidance to federal judges asked to rule on petitions for release under the Act. In particular, the offender must have already served ten years of a ten-year or longer sentence.[ii] Next, to grant modification, the court would be required to first conclude that (1) the offender is no longer a danger to any person or to the community, (2) the offender demonstrates "readiness for re-entry" into the community, and (3) the interests of justice warrant modification. Furthermore, to the extent modification was granted, these individuals would not be unleashed into the community without restrictions. Far from it; any person released under the Act would be placed on supervised release for a statutorily required period.

The Act, as most legislative proposals do, included findings. First, the Act was based on a finding that the size of the U.S. jail and prison population is severely out of proportion with the U.S. population as a whole.[iii] While America is home to 5 percent of the world's population, we have over 20 percent of the world's prison population, with over 2.2 million people behind bars.[iv] Second, our incarceration rate is now five to ten times higher than that of our industrialized peers.[v] And third, people "age out of crime" around twenty-five years old.[vi] It is no coincidence that brain functions, such as "impulse control, emotional regulation, delayed gratification, and resistance to peer influence"[vii]—all of which directly impact one's inclination to engage in criminal and antisocial behavior—are believed to continue into, but not beyond, one's mid-twenties. Indeed, according to Mauer:

> A longstanding finding in the criminology literature is that involvement in criminal activity is strongly dependent on age, an outcome that cuts across race and class lines. Increased involvement in crime begins in the mid-teen years and rises sharply, but for a relatively short period of time. For most crimes, these rates of involvement begin declining by a person's early to mid-twenties and continue on a downward trajectory.[viii]

For all of these reasons, it seemed perfectly sensible to empower federal judges—the same group we trust to make detention and release decisions daily—to assess whether someone who has previously been convicted of a crime now displays the hallmarks of rehabilitation that warrant release. Right? So you would think. The Act is still pending before the Senate Judiciary Committee.

A similar proposal by the Washington, DC, city council—one vigorously opposed by prosecutors—appeared to be perpetually stalled.[ix] Why? Because at some point, we embraced the intensely punitive sentencing regime that characterizes our criminal justice system as a necessary and effective way of addressing criminality. We continue to do so, even in the face of proof that "increasingly lengthy prison terms do not advance public safety,"[x] and proof that "victims prefer a justice system that focuses more on rehabilitation than punishment."[xi]

The common denominator between resistance to the decarceral measures proposed in response to COVID-19 and other decarceral efforts such as the Second Look Act is our widespread disregard for the humanity of those incarcerated, whether they are detained pretrial or "incapacitated" post-conviction. As that young, insightful GW law student recognized, there are countless ways in which the system dehumanizes the accused, from their arrest through trial, particularly when the accused is poor, Black, brown, and/or uneducated. This dehumanization ranges from the heinous conditions that exist within our jails to the seemingly minute, but common, prosecutorial tactic of refusing to reference the defendant by his given name.

Yet we know that prosecutors, judges, and police alike are capable of acknowledging the humanity of the accused when the accused happens to be rich, White, educated and/or politically connected. Prosecutors rarely request detention in white-collar cases, and often allow the accused to avoid the indignity of a formal arrest by agreeing to allow self-surrender. Judges routinely decline to impose significant liberty restraints in such cases. For example, I once prosecuted a bribery case in which the defendant had paid almost $50,000 in bribes to a tax official in exchange for eliminating his tax liability. The maximum statutory penalty for the offense was 15 years in prison. Despite my representations that the individual was a flight risk, the judge declined to impose so much as GPS monitoring (e.g., an ankle bracelet). In a similar vein, the world observed a highly unusual display of humanity and compassion towards Amber Guyger, the White police officer who murdered Botham Jean in his home[xii] when, after sentencing, the trial judge honored Guyger's request for a hug.[xiii] Many critics "questioned whether a [B]lack defendant would have been shown the same compassion."[xiv]

Rather than repudiating these acts of humanity, I submit that we should normalize them so that mercy is no longer contingent on class, wealth, education, status, and race; so that mercy is systemic. So, what role does the prosecutor play as it relates to the normalization of humanity toward the accused? I struggle to put my thoughts into words even as I write this. After more than five years as a prosecutor, having attended dozens of trainings on prosecutorial ethics and best practices, I cannot remember any instance in which it was conveyed that prosecutors have an obligation to acknowledge the humanity of the accused or, at the very least, not undermine it.

Being both prosecutor and prosecuted has underscored the myriad ways in which the U.S. criminal justice system degrades, devalues, and discards those who get caught up within it. I have personally experienced and observed—both as prosecutor and the prosecuted—the harsh and dehumanizing impact of the "us v. them" mentality that infects criminal justice. "Us v. them" is nothing new. It is a mentality that often emerges where differences lie, and where opportunity exists to exploit the less powerful and the disadvantaged. If you have ever been the underdog, or ever struggled to be seen as equal, you know what it means to be "them".

"Us v. them" led colonizers to colonize. "Us v. them" condoned segregated schools. "Us v. them" birthed laws against gay marriage, and continues to minimize the victimization of our transgender population. "Us v. them" so permeates our criminal justice system that it causes prosecutors—who by all accounts, have the greatest ability to rebalance the scales of justice—to sit by, idly squandering that power, behaving as the parrots of detached legislators and pawns of a patently unjust system. Being "them" has forced me to see these realities more clearly than one can see them from government counsel's table.

Some might argue that a prosecutor's obligation to uphold

the humanity of the accused is fulfilled by simply following the rules, principles, and guidelines that govern fair prosecution. For example, in the aftermath of George Floyd's slaying, I worked with several other USAO-DC prosecutors to identify and remedy racial inequity within our office and within our methods of prosecution. Our efforts included a survey that asked participants, amongst other things, whether we ought to examine ways in which our methods of prosecution contribute to racial inequalities. One participant responded:

> It's unnecessary. [The question] erroneously assumes that methods of prosecution cause racial inequality. Our job is to prosecute crime with integrity and fairness. If we do that (which we already do), our actions will lead to justice, not racial inequality.

Certainly this individual needs a crash course on the evolution of the American Criminal Justice System, and the various ways in which mass-incarceration mirrors "earlier forms of social control."[xv] Indeed, no prosecutor should consider herself qualified or worthy of her power without understanding the context and history of the institution she represents. Alexander's "The New Jim Crow," and DuVernay's film "13th" ought to be a part of every prosecutors' basic training program or, at the very least, on every current or aspiring prosecutors reading- and watch-list.[xvi] The history of our criminal justice system aside, there is considerable leeway in how a prosecutor exercises her discretion within the parameters of the rules, principles, and guidelines that govern integrity and fairness. Accordingly, behaving in a way that reaffirms the humanity of the accused must require something more. Indeed, Professor Marc Howard cautions that:

We, as a society, must leave politics and venom aside and ask ourselves how we treat our fellow citizens and human beings. How would we want our friends, family members, and even ourselves to experience punishment for a terrible mistake?[xvii]

He adds that many of today's criminal justice reformers "saw the light" after sitting behind bars and "experiencing firsthand the humanity and suffering that lies within prison walls."[xviii] Perhaps that really is what it takes. Perhaps, if all prosecutors experienced one night in jail, they would be less likely to view ten years as too little time to warrant review under the Second Look Act. They might understand that it is completely conceivable for ten years' incarceration to accomplish the criminal justice system's objectives of punishment, deterrence, rehabilitation, and incapacitation. Perhaps, if more prosecutors had experienced just a few hours behind bars, they would have been more inclined to accept and implement sensible decarceral proposals in response to COVID-19, rather than arguing—as was done in some cases—that the defendant was equally at risk of contracting the disease whether detained or released into the community.

To the extent you believe that the ability to bring about meaningful change rests with elected and appointed prosecutors, and that line prosecutors are too constrained by the legislature, precedent, and internal policy to have real impact, I would argue that every act of humanity towards one defendant adds legitimacy to the system as a whole. Disclosing every piece of information that you would want to have, in the time frame within which you would want to receive it, were you the person charged, is an act of humanity. Holding law enforcement partners accountable when they overstep and undermine the rights of citizens who have simply elected to use a public street or sidewalk is an act of humanity. Fighting for a sentence below the proposed guidelines range, when justice so requires, is an act of humanity. Because doing nothing, when you can't do everything, is the surest way to be a part of the problem rather than its solution.

CONCLUSION

*Believe That You Are Best Equipped to
Inspire Long-Lasting Change*

In *Terry v. Ohio*, the U.S. Supreme Court sanctioned a practice called "stop and frisk"—the hotly debated and widely known ability of an officer to frisk, or "pat down" the outer clothing of a person the officer suspects of criminal activity. In the decision, the Court was not oblivious to the fact that granting police officers such power over individuals they subjectively deemed suspicious could lend itself to widespread abuse. The court fully acknowledged the pitfalls inherent to granting that level of discretion to police officers who, like all of us, suffer from implicit and stereotype bias. From the text of the decision, it is clear that Justice Warren believed he was striking the difficult, but necessary, balance between promoting public safety and protecting against unconstitutional indignities.

Indeed, Justice Warren noted that the exclusionary rule—which requires that evidence obtained in violation of the Fourth Amendment be excluded from criminal trials—is "powerless" to prevent against the inevitable abuses of "stop and frisk." He concluded that, if a good-faith, legitimate, law enforcement purpose was not the impetus for the encounter, the exclusionary rule could not be a meaningful deterrent. He recognized that "[t]he wholesale harassment by certain elements of the police community, of which minority groups, particularly Negroes, frequently complain, will not be stopped by the exclusion of any evidence from any criminal trial."[i] Accordingly, the esteemed jurist welcomed the use of "other remedies" capable of "curtailing abuses for which exclusion may prove inappropriate" and inadequate.[ii]

While the decision was silent on what those other remedies might be, I submit to you that the justice-minded, transformational, prosecutor—prepared and equipped to be a servant of the law—is the remedy. If mass incarceration and a system that devalues, debases, and perpetuates injustice against the Black, brown, poor, and underserved is the illness, then the woke prosecutor, trained early and often on her mandate, is the cure. If the prosecutor is single-handedly the most powerful actor in the criminal justice system, she must lead the next wave of reform.

We often hear prosecutors proclaim that the ability to do justice (i.e., to do what is right) drew them to the role of prosecutor. However, I've learned that "doing justice" is subjective, and differs depending on the life you have lived. For example, when outrage following the murder of George Floyd resulted in arrests of looters and protesters, self-acclaimed justice-minded prosecutors maintained different approaches on how prosecutorial discretion should be exercised in dealing with those cases. It is simply impossible to create a space in which all prosecutors agree on what justice looks like for every case and under every factual scenario—and that is not the goal. The goal is to encourage critical thinking and discussion, and to educate line prosecutors on the magnitude of their power. The goal is for every prosecutor, everywhere, to take ownership of the way in which every choice they make, no matter how mundane it may be in the course of their many and varied prosecutorial tasks, affects life and liberty. We cannot continue to carry out our prosecutorial function unaware of, or unconcerned with, the realities that inform the cases that come across our desks. Crime does not occur in a vacuum. Neither can prosecution.

People often asked me, "Why prosecution and not defense? Do you enjoy putting Black bodies in jail?" I'd often respond, "I don't put people in jail, judges do that." After five years as a prosecutor, I know that simply isn't true, and after reading this book, so do you. Acceptance is an important step of recovery; and if our system is to recover, prosecutors must accept the roles we have played in perpetuating the injustices of today—whether knowingly or not. Ignorance is bliss, but those who know better must do better. As Justice Thurgood Marshall declared just over thirty years ago, with respect to the U.S. Constitution, for "two hundred years it has slowly, through our efforts, grown more durable, more expansive, and more just. But it cannot protect us if we lack the courage, and the self-restraint, to protect ourselves.iii

Transforming the American criminal justice system will require both courage and restraint—courage to use our voices on behalf of those who have made mistakes; and restraint to avoid conflating the accused with the conduct charged. It will require a new framework, and a new type of justice ambassador—one so powerful that she is often vilified. But guided by the *gray*, she can change the narrative. She need only be brave enough to use her voice, her power, and her platform for good, in pursuit of justice—not justice for some, or just for the privileged and politically connected; not justice merely for those of impeccable character, or the ones she favors; but justice for all. As profoundly explained by James Baldwin:

> [I]f one really wishes to know how justice is administered in a country, one does not question the policemen, the

lawyers, the judges, or the protected members of the middle class. One goes to the unprotected [;] ask the wretched how they fare in the halls of justice, and then you will know, not whether or not the country is just, but whether or not it has any love for justice, or any concept of it. It is certain, in any case, that ignorance, allied with power, is the most ferocious enemy justice can have.[iv]

Consider yourself now armed. You have fine-tuned your compass. If you are a prosecutor or an aspiring one, you have your Blueprint. You know how to identify the *gray*. For others, you now understand the extent of the prosecutors' power, and how to identify the truly justice-minded candidates on your local ballot. Whatever your venue—the courtroom or the polls—go forth and be bold; be informed; be transformational.

EPILOGUE

I wrote the opening chapters of this book on the drive from New York to Washington, D.C. after that fateful Thanksgiving weekend. What began as a cathartic, journal-entry blossomed into something much bigger; much bigger than my story and far bigger than me. I am humbled by those who took the time to review all or part of the 45,000+ words included here—Oluseyi, Allana, Kenya, Joseph, Phillipa, and Cary. Your feedback convinced me that I had something the world should see. I am most grateful to God for putting these words on my heart—a pre-requisite to their inclusion on these pages.

I have since resigned from my role at the U.S. Attorney's Office. Ironically, I left prosecution for the same reason that I entered—my desire to have an impact. I chose prosecution over defense work because I knew that, as a defense attorney, my primary consideration would be my client. As a prosecutor, however, I would be expected and invited to consider all stakeholders when deciding what justice ought to look like in any case. By virtue of the job description alone, I knew that I could have more impact as an AUSA than as a member of the defense bar. However, that changed with the birth of this book, which I believe can impact more cases, dockets, and courtrooms than I ever could as a single prosecutor.

Despite my very personal decision to leave prosecution, I continue to believe that justice-minded prosecutors are the key to criminal justice transformation. In the wake of the deaths of George Floyd, Breonna Taylor, and Ahmaud Arbery, I organized a working group of Black prosecutors within my former office. We joined forces to develop data-driven solutions to combat internal and external inequities that had infected our office and the cases that we handled; solutions we would ultimately share with office leadership. Through our work, we convinced the front-office that the Felon-in-Possession Initiative, as it then-existed, was both racist and ineffective. Together, we pressured senior leadership to re-evaluate the way that prosecutors are trained to interact with the communities they serve. Together, we encouraged a data-driven approach to restorative justice, and the development of a robust implicit bias training program. In short, we started a movement;[i] so can you, should you adopt a mindset of service, and seek to leave the system better than you found it.

However, justice-minded prosecutors cannot go at it alone. Prosecutors' offices around the country must recognize that the "sink or swim" initiation method has failed. It has failed the prosecutor, the victim, the defendant, and—most importantly—it has failed to pass constitutional muster. New prosecutors need early and extensive training on their mandate—the type of training that is not facilitated by budget cuts. Yet DOJ's 2021 federal program budget reduces funding for the Innovative Prosecutions Initiative from $8 million to $5 million,[ii] while increasing funding for Project Safe Neighborhoods ("PSN")—the program that financed the FIP-Initiative—from $20 million to $40 million.[iii] We must do better.

I truly hope and expect that we will see a shift in priorities following the transition of national leadership; but we do not have to wait. We can all start being transformational now. We can start taking small steps toward the justice system we want to see, now. We can require an individualized approach to each case and each defendant, now. Prosecutors can make a decision to honor their *Berger*[iv] mandate now.

In the words of the poet who occupied that 7th precinct N.Y.C. cell before me—the time to set injustice ablaze and to "burn it down" is now.

ENDNOTES

INTRODUCTION

i   Ronald F. Wright and Kay L. Levine, "The Cure for Young Prosecutors' Syndrome", *Arizona Law Review*, Vol. 56:4, at 1066-1128, https://arizonalawreview.org/pdf/56-4/56arizlrev1065.pdf

ii   Bryan Stevenson, *Just Mercy: A story of Justice and Redemption*, Random House Books, New York (2014), 40, iBooks.

iii   Michelle Alexander, *The New Jim Crow: Mass Incarceration in the Age of Colorblindedness*, New Press, New York (2012), 174, iBooks (hereinafter "The New Jim Crow").

iv   *Ibid.*

PART ONE

CHAPTER 2

i   Marc Morjé Howard, *Unusually Cruel: Prisons, Punishment, and the Real America Exceptionalism*, Figure 1.4 (2017), IBook, https://books.apple.com/us/book/unusually-cruel/id1237656058 (hereinafter "Unusually Cruel").

ii   Prison Policy Initiative, "Policing Women: Race and gender disparities in police stops, searches, and use of force" (May 14, 2019), *available at: https://www.prisonpolicy.org/blog/2019/05/14/policingwomen/*

iii   Nicholas Fandos, "A Study Documents the Paucity of Black Elected Prosecutors: Zero in Most States," *New York Times*, (July 7, 2015), https://www.nytimes.com/2015/07/07/us/a-study-documents-the-paucity-of-black-elected-prosecutors-zero-in-most-states.html

iv   Michelle S. Jacobs, *The Violent State: Black Women's Invisible Struggle Against Police Violence,* (Nov. 2017):65, https://scholarship.law.wm.edu/cgi/viewcontent.cgi?article=1462&context=wmjowl (hereinafter "The Violent State").

v   Jacobs, "The Violent State," 65.

vi   Jacobs, "The Violent State," 45-46 ("Stereotypes about Black women developed during this historical era are still dominant in state policy today. . . . [a]ll aspects of criminal law have embedded the stereotypes as the normative foundation for how government evaluates, judges, and punishes Black women.")

CHAPTER 3

i   *Ecclesiastes* 3:1-8 (KJV, 1611).

CHAPTER 4

i   *Arizona v. Gant*, 556 U.S. 332, 343-44 (2009).

ii   *Ibid.*, 343-45.

iii *Ibid.*, 342-43.

iv   *Ibid.*, 43–44.

v   *Ibid.*, 342.

CHAPTER 6

i   *Terry v. Ohio*, 392 U.S. 1, 14 (1968).

CHAPTER 8

i   David Montgomery, "Sandra Bland, It Turns Out, Filmed Traffic Stop Confrontation Herself," *New York Times* (May 7, 2019), https://www.nytimes.com/2019/05/07/us/sandra-bland-video-brian-encinia.html.

ii   *Ibid.*

PART TWO

CHAPTER 16

i   Brief of the District of Columbia as *Amicus Curiea* Supporting
        Petitioner, *United States v. John Victor Reed,* No. 19-CR-00093
        (EGS), at *14 (D.D.C. Apr. 21, 2020) (DE 39), *available at: https://
        oag.dc.gov/sites/default/files/2020-04/FIP-Amicus-US-v-Reed.pdf*

ii   U.S. Sentencing Commission, "Quick facts – Felon in Possession of
        a firearm," (last visited Dec. 12, 2020), https://www.ussc.gov/sites/
        default/files/pdf/research-and-publications/quick-facts/Felon_In_
        Possession_FY18.pdf.

iii   Peter   Hermann,   Dana Hedgpeth,   and   Justin   Wm.   Moyer,
        "Homicides spike in District as shootings become more lethal, police
        say", December 31st, 2018, https://www.washingtonpost.com/local/
        public-safety/homicides-spike-in-district-as-shootings-become-
        more-lethal-police-say/2018/12/31/a781b28e-02c6-11e9-b5df-
        5d3874f1ac36_story.html?utm_term=.2c0944198339.

iv   *Ibid.*

v   *Ibid.*

CHAPTER 17

i   Jonathan Blanks, "Thin Blue Lies: How Pretextual Stops Undermine
        Police Legitimacy", *Case Western Reserve Law Review* (2016), *https://
        scholarlycommons.law.case.edu/cgi/viewcontent.cgi?article=4660&conte
        xt=caselrev.*

ii   *Ibid.,* 935.

PART THREE

i   *Berger v. United States,* 295 U.S. 78, 88 (1935).

ii   Angela Davis, "The Power and Discretion of the American Prosecutor,"
        Droit et Cultures, (2005): 49, https://journals.openedition.org/

droitcultures/1580?lang=en

iii   Michelle Alexander, *The New Jim Crow: Mass Incarceration in the Age of Colorblindedness*, (2012), 174, iBook

iv   Alexander, "The New Jim Crow," 174.

v   *Ibid.,* 345.

vi   A.W Purdue.: "The Transformative Impact of World War II", *European History Online* (EGO), *Leibniz Institute of European History (IEG) Mainz* 2016: 04-18, http://www.ieg-ego.eu/purduea-2016-en URN: urn:nbn:de:0159-2016041204.

LESSON 1

i   Marc Mauer and Meda Chesney-Lind, eds., *Invisible Punishment: The Collateral Consequences of Mass Imprisonment* (New York: The New Press, 2002), 5, citing *American Bar Association, Task Force on Collateral Sanctions*, "Introduction, Proposed Standards on Collateral Sanctions and Administrative Disqualification of Convicted Persons,"(Jan. 18, 2002).

LESSON 3

i   *Gerstein v. Pugh*, 420 U.S. 103, 118 (1975).

ii   *Ibid.*

iii   *Ibid.*, 114 (citing 18 U.S.C. ss 3146(a)(2), (5)).

iv   *County of Riverside v. McLaughlin*, 500 U.S. 44 (1991) (Scalia, J. dissent).

v   *Ibid.*

vi   *United States v. Salerno*, 481 U.S. 739 (1987).

vii   N.Y. Crim. Proc. Law §150.20 (McKinney).

viii   N.Y. Crim. Proc. §159.20 Law (McKinney), excluding Class A, B, C, D felonies, sex offenses, and escape-related crimes.

ix   Karen Dolan and Jodi L. Carr, "The Poor Get Prison: The Alarming

Spread of the Criminalization of Poverty, at 6 (2015), https://ips-dc. org/wp-content/uploads/2015/03/IPS-The-Poor-Get-Prison-Final. pdf

x   *Ibid.*, 7.

LESSON 5

i   "N.Y.C. Board of Corrections, pre-Sentence Reports: Utility or Futility", *Fordham Law Review*, (1973), https://ir.lawnet.fordham. edu/cgi/viewcontent.cgi?article=1037&context=ulj.

ii   Wright and Levine, *supra,* at 1071.

LESSON 6

i   Jessica Pishko, "Prosecutors Are Banding Together to Prevent Criminal-Justice Reform," *The Nation*, October 18, 2017, https:// www.thenation.com/article/archive/prosecutors-are-banding-together-to-prevent-criminal-justice-reform/.

ii   Howard, "Unusually Cruel," 96.

iii Alexander, "The New Jim Crow," 156.

iv   *Santobello v. New York*, 404 U.S. 257, 261 (1971).

v   "Memorandum on Department Charging and Sentencing Policy," Department *of Justice*, 1, https://www.justice.gov/opa/press-release/ file/965896/download.

vi   Howard, " Unusually Cruel," Chapter 2.

LESSON 7

i   *Brady v. Maryland*, 373 U.S. 83, 87 (1963).

ii   *Ibid.* at 87–88.

iii *Berger v. United States*, 295 U.S. 78, 88 (1935).

iv   *Brady,* 373 U.S. at 88.

v   JaneAnne Murray, "The Brady Battle," *National Association of*

Criminal Defense Lawyers, (2013), https://www.nacdl.org/Article/May2013-TheBradyBattle.

vi   Jessica Brand and Ethan Brown, "US Attorney's Office that Prosecuted Inauguration Day Protesters Has History of Misconduct Findings", *The Appeal*, (2018), https://theappeal.org/us-attorneys-office-that-prosecuted-inauguration-day-protesters-has-long-history-of-misconduct/

vii *United States v. Celis*, 608 F.3d 818, 833 (D.C. Cir. 2010).

LESSON 9

i   Alexander, "The New Jim Crow," 340.

LESSON 10

i   Marc Mauer, "Long-Term Sentences: Time to Reconsider the Scale of Punishment," *The Sentencing Project*, (2018), 114, https://www.sentencingproject.org/publications/long-term-sentences-time-reconsider-scale-punishment/ (hereinafter "Long-Term Sentences."

ii   Mauer, "Long-Term Sentences," 114.

iii Mauer, *"Long-Term Sentences," 113-127.*

iv   D.C. Code Section 401.

v   Howard, "Unusually Cruel," 130.

vi   *Ibid.*, 156-57.

vii *Ibid.*, 130.

viii *Ibid.*, 133.

ix   *Ibid.*

x   Howard, "Unusually Cruel," 279-80.

xi   Paul Gendreau, Claire Goggin, and Francis T. Cullen, "The Effects of Prison Sentences on Recidivism," *Public Works and Government Services Canada* (1999), 18, https://www.prisonpolicy.org/scans/e199912.htm.

xii   Howard, "Unusually Cruel," 280.

xiii *Ibid.*

xiv *Ibid.,* 187 (internal quotations omitted).

xv Mauer, "Long-Term Sentences," 113-127.

LESSON 11

i   S. 2146, 116th Congress. § 2 (2019), *available at:* https://www.congress.gov/bill/116th-congress/senate-bill/2146/text.

ii S. 2146, 116th Congress, § 3.

iii S. 2146, 116th Congress, § 2.

iv S. 2146, 116th Congress, § 2.

v S. 2146, 116th Congress, § 2.

vi S. 2146, 116th Congress, § 2.

vii Laurence Steinberg, "Risk Taking in Adolescence," *New Perspectives from Brain and Behavioral Science*: 56, http://citeseerx.ist.psu.edu/viewdoc/download?doi=10.1.1.519.7099&rep=rep1&type=pdf.

viii Mauer, "Long-Term Sentences," 122.

ix On December 15, 2020, the D.C. Council approved the Second Look Amendment Act, which allows any offender convicted of a crime committed before age 25 to petition a judge for early release after serving 15 years of their sentence.

x *Ibid., 118.*

xi *Crime Survivors Speak: The First-Ever National Survey of Victims' Views on Safety and Justice* (Oakland, CA: Alliance for Safety and Justice, 2019), https://allianceforsafetyandjustice.org/wp-content/uploads/2019/04/Crime-Survivors-Speak-Report-1.pdf.

xii Sarah Mervosh and Nicholas Bogel-Burroughs, "Amber Guyger's Judge Gave her a Bible and Hug. Did That Cross a Line?" The New York Times (Oct. 4, 2019), https://www.nytimes.com/2019/10/04/us/amber-guyger-judge-tammy-kemp-hug.html?auth=login-email&login=email.

xiii   *Ibid.*

xiv   *Ibid.*

xv   13th-The Film, Ava DuVernay (2016), http://www.avaduvernay. com/13th; Alexander, "The New Jim Crow," (2012), iBook.

xvi   *Ibid.*

xvii Howard, "Unusually Cruel", 529.

xviii *Ibid.*

CONCLUSION

i   *Terry v. Ohio*, 392 U.S. 1, 14–15, 88 S. Ct. 1868, 1876 (1968).

ii   *Ibid.*

iii   *United States v. Salerno*, 481 U.S. 739, 767 (1987).

iv   James Baldwin, *No Name in the Street* (1972), 149.

EPILOGUE

i   Keith L. Alexander, "32 Black federal prosecutors in Washington have a plan to make the criminal justice system more fair," *The Washington Post,* (2020), https://www.washingtonpost.com/local/public-safety/32-black-federal-prosecutors-in-washington-have-a-plan-to-make-the-criminal-justice-system-more-fair/2020/09/05/1774d646-ed4b-11ea-ab4e-581edb849379_story.html.

ii   U.S. Department of Justice FY 2021 Performance Budget, Office of Programs (Feb. 2020), https://www.justice.gov/doj/page/file/1246736/download

iii   *Ibid.*, 87.

iv   *Berger v. United States*, 295 U.S. 78 (1935).

ABOUT THE AUTHOR

PHOTO BY: © Photograph by Tre Lynn
https://www.trelynnpro.com/

Bianca M. Forde is a seasoned litigator, fearless advocate, and justice warrior. After spending nearly one decade representing global entities in high-stakes, commercial disputes, Bianca joined the ranks of federal prosecution motivated by a desire to "do justice." As an Assistant United States Attorney for the District of Columbia, Bianca investigated a wide-variety of cases, ranging from violent crime to public corruption. She has served as the Eastern Regional Director (2019-20), and Vice-President of Legislative and Social Action (2020-21) for the National Black Prosecutors Association, where she is focused on transforming the narrative around criminal justice by emphasizing the power of the prosecutor to undo systemic imbalances. She is an avid traveler, a karaoke enthusiast, and a proud member of Delta Sigma Theta Sorority, Incorporated. Bianca received her Bachelor of Arts in Political Science and African-American Studies (minor) from Duke University in Durham, North Carolina, and her Juris Doctor degree from Boston College Law School in Newton, Massachusetts. This is her first book.

Made in the USA
Middletown, DE
01 November 2023

41587696R00123